make it
stick:

70 Practical Ideas for Sermons, Board Meetings, Small Group Gatherings, and Holidays

Group

Loveland, Colorado
www.group.com

Group resources actually work!

This Group resource helps you focus on **"The 1 Thing®"**— a life-changing relationship with Jesus Christ. "The 1 Thing" incorporates our **R.E.A.L.** approach to ministry. It reinforces a growing friendship with Jesus, encourages long-term learning, and results in life transformation, because it's:

Relational
Learner-to-learner interaction enhances learning and builds Christian friendships.

Experiential
What learners experience through discussion and action sticks with them up to 9 times longer than what they simply hear or read.

Applicable
The aim of Christian education is to equip learners to be both hearers and doers of God's Word.

Learner-based
Learners understand and retain more when the learning process takes into consideration how they learn best.

Visit our Web site: **www.group.com**

Credits
Compiling Editor: Mike Nappa
Editor: Candace McMahan
Chief Creative Officer: Joani Schultz
Copy Editor: Ann Jahns
Art Director/Cover Art Director: Jeff Storm
Cover Photographer: Rodney Stewart
Production Manager: DeAnne Lear
Interior Designer: Pamela Poll

Unless otherwise indicated, all Scripture quotations are taken from the *Holy Bible*, New Living Translation, copyright © 1996, 2004. Used by permission of Tyndale House Publishers, Inc., Carol Stream, Illinois 60188. All rights reserved.

Some of the activities in this book are drawn from sources previously published by Group Publishing, Inc. "Posture of Prayer," "Sweet Hearts," "Get Off My Pew!" "No Random Gift," "Free at Last," "Wedded Bliss," "Dressed for Winter," "Spring Cleaning for the Soul," "Happy New Life," and "God's Rest" copyright © 1995 Nappaland Communications, Inc. All rights reserved. Reprinted by permission from *Bore No More* by Mike and Amy Nappa. For more information or to contact the authors, access the Internet magazine for families at www.Nappaland.com.

Library of Congress Cataloging-in-Publication Data
Make it stick : 70 practical ideas for sermons, board meetings, small group gatherings, and holidays / with an introduction by Alan Nelson, executive editor of Rev! Magazine ; [editor, Candace McMahan ; compiling editor, Mike Nappa]. -- 1st American pbk. ed.
    p. cm.
Includes indexes.
ISBN 978-0-7644-3557-7 (pbk. : alk. paper)
1. Communication--Religious aspects--Christianity. 2. Pastoral theology.
I. McMahan, Candace. II. Nappa, Mike, 1963-
BV4319.M25 2007
251'.08--dc22
                                2007009149
ISBN 978-0-7644-3557-7
10 9 8 7 6 5 4 3 2 1 16 15 14 13 12 11 10 09 08 07
Printed in the United States of America.

People retain only 10
percent of what they hear,
but 90 percent of
what they experience.

contents

Part One: The Case for Experiential Learning

Part Two: The Experiences

Make Your Message Stick...*From the Pulpit*

Make Your Message Stick...*In Pastoral Staff and Board Meetings*

Make Your Message Stick...*In Adult Small Group and Sunday School Settings*

Make Your Message Stick...*On Holidays and Special Occasions*

Index

the case for experiential learning

make your sermon 90% stickier!

by Alan Nelson, Executive Editor of REV! Magazine

*"Education is not the filling of a pail,
but the lighting of a fire."*

—William Butler Yeats

Trouble in the Faith Factory

Imagine you're the CEO of a computer factory. One day, while touring the assembly line, you notice that nine out of every 10 computers are dropping off the conveyor belt, crashing onto the floor. Aghast, you sprint to the emergency switch and shut down the line. "What's going on?" you shout. "Why isn't somebody doing something to prevent this?" If you were in charge of the assembly line, you'd do something about it, wouldn't you?

Now move from the computer factory to the sanctuary. By the time your people reach the exit of your church, they've already forgotten over 90 percent of what you just invested more than half of your work-week preparing. Let's say the typical pastor in America works 50 hours per week, 25 of these hours on sermon preparation and presentation. Research numbers vary, but based on a $40,000 annual salary and over 300,000 churches, that equates to more than $115,000,000 per week in message preparation. In light of cultural trends and church growth in America, I would argue that we are not seeing a positive return on this significant investment.

What can we do to make our investment yield higher returns, assuming that the more God's Word lingers in the minds and hearts of our people, the more their lives will be transformed?

Active Learning

There is a proven way to significantly increase the residual effect of our sermons. It is a method that Jesus often implemented as well as the approach that organizations such as Group (the publisher of this book) and the American Society of Training and Development utilize. Educators refer to it as active learning. And it works: research indicates that people remember 5 to 10 percent of what they hear but 80 to 90 percent of what they experience.

How Did Jesus Teach?

Whether he was mentoring one-on-one, instructing a small group, or teaching the masses, Jesus employed a variety of teaching methods: lecture, parables (with and without explanation), visual aids, the Socratic method, and active learning. Powerful examples of active learning include Jesus' turning water into wine (John 2:1-11), instructing one of his disciples to catch a fish and pull a coin out of its mouth (Matthew 17:24-26), healing a blind man by mixing his spit into the dirt and making mud (John 9:1-11), cursing a fig tree and causing it to wither in front of the disciples (Matthew 21:18-22), inviting Peter to walk on water (Matthew 14:25-33), and encouraging Thomas to touch his side (John 20:27). In all these examples, he moved his listeners beyond listening into the realm of *experiencing* the truths he wanted them to understand.

When you think about it, Jesus' primary discipleship method was a three-year experiential model whereby the Twelve did life with him, resulting in the most effective transformation of a single small group in recorded history! While we can't embark on three-year camping trips with our people, we *can* use brief, experiential learning events within the context of worship services, board retreats, staff meetings, and small groups to move them toward more profound learning.

How Do Business Leaders Teach?

The American Society for Training and Development is a 70,000-member professional organization that trains the trainers of American and international corporations, including Fortune 500 companies. When I registered for ASTD's certification, I assumed I'd be receiving a covey of training tools with powerful statistics, PowerPoint slides, and notes on effective education. Instead I received two days of nonstop active-learning examples and experiences. Big business has discovered that active learning is not just for public school students; it is an effective way for adults to acquire vital job information. Churches would do well to discover what their corporate colleagues, if not their lead Teacher, know about how people learn.

The Importance of Interaction

In an educational study, during each of five lectures, a teacher paused for two minutes at three different times. During the pauses, students worked in pairs to discuss and rework their notes, and no interaction occurred between the instructor and students. At the end of each lecture, students were given three minutes to write down everything they could remember from the lecture; then, 12 days after the last lecture, the students were given a 65-item, multiple-choice test to measure long-term retention.

The researchers also tracked a control group, which attended the same lectures but wasn't offered the pauses, and this group was similarly tested.

The same research test was conducted twice, and the results were striking and consistent: Students who interacted at various points throughout the lectures did significantly better on both the free recall and the comprehensive test. In fact, the magnitude of the difference in mean scores between the two groups was large enough to make a difference of two letter grades![1]

Do you realize what this means? If we talk six minutes *less* and engage in an activity that reinforces what we teach, people will learn *far more*.

How Do Pastors Teach?

More and more pastors are trying to make their teaching more meaningful and in the process are rediscovering their roots in the early church. They're communicating through story, experience, and word pictures. The rise of the arts in the church is also a move in this direction, since the arts touch us emotionally, making our messages more memorable. Through movie clips, high-tech sound systems, candles, and mood

---

1. K.L. Ruhl, C.A. Hughes, and P.J. Schloss, "Using the pause procedure to enhance lecture recall," Teacher Education and Special Education [Winter 1987], 14-18.

lighting, the church is intuitively embracing active-learning principles.

Even so, the concept of active learning still isn't on the typical pastor's radar. If Jesus and top trainers use this method, why don't most of us in ministry? I can think of at least five reasons:

1. We've not seen this method modeled. Most of us in church leadership have assumed that the best way to teach is to mimic what we've experienced in public education, seminaries, pastor conferences, and church services. We rarely question whether this is the most effective way to teach.

But if we bear in mind that the goal of Christian education is not content acquisition but life transformation, our methods will change. Remember, for a large part of his ministry, Jesus had only 12 students, and they accompanied him on a three-year experiential journey.

2. Using traditional lecture methods, the pastor gets to be the star. Traditional teaching methods make the teacher the center of attention. An underlying message is "Look at me. Listen to what I have to say. I'm in charge. I'm educated, the authority on this subject. You need what I know." But this approach is *teacher* based, not *learner* based.

The sage-on-the-stage mindset is a fact of life that even the most humble of us wrestles with, if we're honest. By designing messages and selecting methods that fit our teaching style instead of our listeners' learning style, we put ourselves first.

3. Active learning requires more work. Surveys show that the one facet of their calling pastors enjoy most is preparing and delivering sermons. That's one reason more than half of the typical pastor's workweek is invested in message prep. Most of us find pleasure in being sequestered in our studies, removed from the fray, preparing the spiritual meal of the week for our flocks. While much sermon preparation is constructive, it is not healthy if it lulls us into avoiding the hard work of ministry: understanding where our listeners are in their lives and crafting messages that will truly affect their lives. Designing a one-way message, lecture, or speech is far easier than crafting a compelling experience that moves people from being mere hearers of the Word to doers.

Jesus often pushed the envelope with his audience, asking strategic questions and challenging comfort zones. He called people out of the boat physically, not just intellectually.

4. Active learning is risky. Experiential learning is unpredictable. Neither you nor the participants can predict what the outcome will be.

But surprise is a wonderful part of authentic learning. When people are caught off-guard, they are much more likely to remember the lesson than if they'd seen the point coming from a mile away.

Handing over the learning process to disciples, even in part, is a scary process, for both teacher and student. When Jesus told his disciples he'd be leaving them soon, they were full of anxiety. But to produce true disciples, Jesus knew he had to release them to learn on their own.

> It's not that the Word is sterile; rather, our methods of teaching it are impotent.

5. Active learning expects more of learners. By providing listeners with notes, PowerPoint slides, soft seats, and climate-controlled environments, we may be inadvertently sabotaging congregants' ability to grapple with and internalize the truths we're trying to impart. Are we creating consumers, spiritual spectators who only *think* they're participating? Because we have failed to engage them emotionally, physically, and relationally, are they absorbing less? We leave it up to them to apply what they've learned cognitively, but—let's be honest—how many people really do?

No wonder so many people can attend church for years, gleaning factoids and doctrine, and still fail to mature in their faith or reflect love in their relationships. They haven't internalized the messages they've heard because we've used methods that fail to engage them in dynamic, robust learning.

Lewis Carbone writes in *Clued In*, "If you are considering how you feel *about* Starbucks, you are thinking about the Starbucks brand. If you think about how *you yourself feel* as a result of a visit to a Starbucks, you are relating to the experience…What customers value is the experience. And that's what they associate with the brand."[2] In the context of the local church, good learning has taken place when people leave saying, "Wow, that was a wonderful message." *Great* learning has occurred when people leave saying, "I feel as if I connected with God."

The Big Reason: Bad Experiences

Many pastors have another reason to avoid experiential learning methods: They've had bad experiences with them. Perhaps they took part

2. Lewis Carbone, *Clued In: How to Keep Customers Coming Back Again and Again*, Upper Saddle River, NJ: Financial Times Prentice Hall, 2004, 44.

in a cheesy activity at a camp or retreat or they participated in a poorly executed discussion that left them thinking, "If that's active learning, you can keep it." In order to prevent their own people from suffering through embarrassing moments and heading for the doors as fast as they can say, "Share with your partner," they've given up active-learning methods altogether.

Poor teaching is poor, whether it's done in the context of a lecture or an attempt at active learning. But just because a pastor has had a bad experience with active learning, continuing to deliver forgettable monologues every week is not the answer.

Developing quality active learning experiences is not easy. It requires practice and honing. But it is worth the effort.

Six Elements of Effective Active Learning

To really engage people in authentic learning, a quality active-learning experience should contain all of the following elements:

1. It involves everyone. Sitting in a comfortable seat while listening to a talking head is an easy but lazy way to obtain information. Why not watch television, read a book, or watch a video instead? Moreover, involving only a few people in an active-learning experience will not have much of an effect on the entire congregation. To be truly memorable, the experience should involve *everyone*.

2. It is an adventure. Participants in an active-learning experience don't know

An easy way to remember the elements of authentic learning is through this acrostic Group has developed: **R.E.A.L.**

R.E.A.L. learning is

Relational—We often learn best when we're interacting with others, who provide unique perspectives and insights as well as listening ears to our thoughts in process.

Experiential—Physical interaction that also engages multiple senses cements learning.

Applicable—Good teaching is relevant. It connects ideas with everyday life by focusing on *how* in addition to *what*.

Learner-based—Effective communication begins with an understanding of the audience. That's why Jesus never used canned approaches when explaining the kingdom; rather, when he was speaking to shepherds, he talked about lost sheep; to farmers, vineyards; to fishermen, fishing for men; to a woman fetching water, living water; to philosophers, life's riddles.

what the outcome will be; in fact, even the designer of the activity can't predict the outcome. That's what makes active learning different from an object lesson, the outcome of which is controlled. Participants might respond with laughter, embarrassment, chatter, thoughtfulness, and even tears. Whatever the responses, the learning will be rich.

3. It stands alone as a fun or captivating thing to do with friends. Effective learning activities are intrinsically interesting. They cause participants to want to share the ideas with people outside of church.

4. It evokes emotion. The emotional element is what drives an experience from short-term to long-term memory. When you ask people to reflect on the most memorable times in their lives, they nearly always refer to times of intense emotions, both positive and negative. Just as searing a steak locks in its flavor, emotions serve as the glue that seals learning.

5. It is age-appropriate. One reason pastors reject active-learning methods is that the ones they've experienced were childish or goofy. It is imperative that these experiences genuinely appeal to the age group to which they're directed.

6. It is coupled with strong debriefing and world-class questions. Even a modest time spent reflecting on an activity deepens learning. One of the most valuable benefits of discussions with a partner or a small group is the insight participants gain into *themselves* as a result of articulating their thoughts and feelings. Putting thoughts into words requires next-level thinking. How can we truly know or understand something if we can't begin to articulate it?

Great questions are open-ended; there are no right or wrong answers or simple, one-word responses. Instead, answers are individual and different, depending on the respondent's unique perceptions, knowledge, personality, and experiences. Great questions are never lame, obvious, or leading.

Reminders of Important Truths

When people have a good experience, they want a reminder of it. When they go on vacation or attend a theme park, concert, or camp, they want to take home something that will help them remember the experience. For many it's a photo. For some it's a T-shirt. For others it's a trinket. Physical objects stimulate our memories of important events.

When the people of Israel crossed the Jordan River into the Promised Land, they took a dozen stones from the river bottom and created a monument that would cause future generations to ask why the stones were there (Joshua 4:4-7). Jesus gave new meaning to mud, to fish and small loaves of bread, to water and wine, to ointment, and to an instrument of death. The items became significant because of the meanings attached to them. Throughout biblical history, mundane items took on special meaning when attached to important events and principles.

By giving people simple items symbolizing biblical truths, we can provide daily reminders of those truths.

> People retain only about 10% of what they hear or read, but up to 90% of what they experience.

Creating a Buzz

One beneficial side effect of active learning in the church is that it gets people talking about their Sunday experience throughout the week. They tell their friends, neighbors, associates at work, and relatives about the unusual thing they did in church, or they share the souvenir they took away from the Sunday message. The more people talk about these experiences, the more your church will stand out and the more others will want to visit. Because you've made the Bible relevant to their lives, you've turned spectators into participants, consumers into evangelists.

But Still...

All these considerations aside, when you think about employing new teaching methods in your own church, you may still have reservations. For example, you may be wondering,

Is active learning really feasible in large groups? You might consider employing active-learning techniques in relatively intimate settings such as staff meetings, leadership retreats, and small groups, but you still can't envision using them in typical Sunday morning worship services.

So begin with baby steps. Don't go for the deep end right away. Wade in first; then swim. You'll be amazed at how well people respond if you gradually introduce active learning at nonthreatening levels and then occasionally deepen the involvement. Here are levels you might move through as you gradually introduce your congregation to the idea of active learning:

• **Level 1:** Employ a visual aid, creating a metaphor for a key point.

• **Level 2:** Recruit one or more members of the congregation to demonstrate a point in front of the entire body.

• **Level 3:** Ask everyone to participate in an experience by creating a written or visual aid of their own.

• **Level 4:** Involve everyone in an experience and then ask them to debrief the experience with two, three, or four people sitting near them. The key at first is to acknowledge that people aren't used to this sort of thing and to ask them to give it a try. Comments such as "Now we're going to do something a little different" and "Let's try this and see what happens" will lighten the mood and take some of the awkwardness out of your first few experiments with active learning. It's also important to provide exits so that people don't feel forced to share at levels at which they're uncomfortable.

Especially in "seeker-friendly" churches, won't people be scared away if we ask them to share their thoughts with the strangers sitting next to them? Today's "seekers" are different from those of the 1980s, when the term described people returning to church who desired anonymity. Today's postmodern seeker values experiences and authenticity over anonymity.

Can I really expect my traditional congregation to accept a new—and threatening—method of learning? First, remember that, as the leader of your church, you're its cultural architect. Through your words and actions, you establish the norm for your congregation. If you don't, then you're not doing your job.

Anyone who's been attending church more than five years has an innate problem caused by the reticular activator. This finger-sized portion of the brain actually blocks messages that are deemed familiar and nonthreatening. In essence, when confronted with familiar information, the brain says, "Been there. Done that. Bought the T-shirt." For veterans of the faith to hear old things anew, you *have* to teach differently.

After Getting Your Feet Wet, Take the Plunge

Are there risks? Of course there are. Any dynamic learning process is dangerous. But remember that, when Jesus washed his disciples' feet, he said, "You don't understand now what I am doing, but someday you will" (John 13:7). In the same way, when you lead people through active learning, there will be times when they don't understand why and what you're doing, but when done well, your efforts will be transformational.

If you've measured the results of your preaching over the years and are happy with your congregation's spiritual growth, then by all means keep doing what you've been doing. But if you suspect there might be a better way to grow people into the likeness of Christ, I encourage you to try something different.

Begin simply. As with every new skill, you'll become more adept the more you practice. Use the activities in this book and as you become better at developing your own experiential lessons, your people will increasingly anticipate and welcome them. Include active learning in your repertoire of methods. Transform the way you teach—teach like Jesus.

Further Reading

- American Society for Training and Development, www.astd.org
- Lenderman, Max. *Experience the Message.* New York, NY: Carroll & Graf Publishers, 2006.
- Nelson, Alan. *Creating Messages That Connect.* Loveland, CO: Group Publishing, Inc., 2004. (Free e-book available at www.unforgettables .org.)
- Schultz, Thom and Joani. *Why Nobody Learns Much of Anything at Church: And How to Fix It.* Loveland, CO: Group Publishing, Inc., 1993.

About Alan Nelson

Alan Nelson has a graduate degree in communication psychology and EdD in leadership, is certified by the American Society of Training and Development, was a pastor for 20 years, and is the author of a dozen books, most recently *Coached by Jesus.* He currently serves as the executive editor of Rev! magazine and is the director of pastoral resources at Group.

how to use this book

Congratulations.

If you've read this far, you value authentic, memorable teaching—and you're ready to live out that value in the way you conduct the ministry of your church. So again, congratulations. You're going to make a lasting difference in the lives of the people in your congregation.

In *Make It Stick* you'll find 70 authentic, memorable learning experiences modeled after Jesus' interactive teaching style and designed for use during sermons, pastoral staff and board meetings, adult small-group and Sunday school classes, and holidays and other special occasions. We've compiled winning ideas from several previously published Group resources and added some creative new ideas to round out this collection. Here's what you need to know about how to use this resource...

Illustrate—But Don't Eliminate

The ideas in this book aren't intended to *replace* your sermon or your small-group lesson. Rather, they're meant to *supplement* your teaching, to provide attention-getting, audience-involving, memorable experiences that will make your teaching come alive.

What you'll find here are short (five- to 15-minute) experiential learning activities that you can use to illustrate individual points or themes within your teaching time. Use these ideas at any point during a sermon to really bring home your message. Or use them to open a small group or close a staff meeting. Basically, if it's time to illustrate your point—say, with a story or poem—try using one of these active, audience-involving illustrations instead.

The Letters of Paul

Through his letters (and under the inspiration of the Holy Spirit), the Apostle Paul wrote the bulk of the New Testament, and in so doing, defined Christian theology for all of history. It's no wonder, then, that over the course of a typical year the majority of expository teaching that an American pastor does on the New Testament is invariably drawn from the Pauline epistles:

Romans	Philippians	1 Timothy
1 Corinthians	Colossians	2 Timothy
2 Corinthians	1 Thessalonians	Titus
Galatians	2 Thessalonians	Philemon
Ephesians		

Since we know that you're likely to teach from one (or most) of these books in the coming year, we decided to focus *Make It Stick* on this section of Scripture as well. We hope this focus will help you maximize your teaching potential in the coming months and will be a big help as you prepare for your next sermon series!

If you like what you see here but wish you could also find ideas drawn from the gospels, the non-Pauline epistles, or the Old Testament books, we have many resources that will help. Just check out our Web site, www.group.com, for more information.

About Bible Translations

The ideas in this book use the New Living Translation (NLT) as their default text. However, you can use these ideas with any translation of Scripture that you prefer. You'll just want to double-check the wording of your preferred translation against the wording used in your chosen activity and adjust the terminology accordingly before you present to your audience.

Assessing Emotional Risk Factors in Your Audience

Some of your hearers—particularly in a congregation or other large-group setting—may not be used to interactive learning experiences in the church, and that's OK. The more you incorporate these kinds of teaching techniques into your ministry, the more people will grow comfortable with this type of long-lasting learning method. Still, there is an emotional risk even in something as simple and innately relational as asking an audience member to discuss a thought with a friend. So, to help you assess your congregation's readiness for a specific activity, we've included a "risk rating" with each idea in this book.

Low-risk ideas will typically require minimal involvement from an audience member—such as "Stand up, sit down" or "Write something on a piece of paper"—and will call for only limited or no discussion with others.

Medium-risk ideas will typically call for some kind of discussion or debriefing with a partner or a small group and may ask audience members to move around a bit.

High-risk ideas will be rare—but effective! These activities will usually require a longer-term effort, such as having a small group get together to bake Communion bread, or stretch audience members beyond their comfort zones by, for example, asking some of them to leave the auditorium and return in five minutes with something that reminds them of God.

Because the activities are designed to take place in different settings, you'll notice that there is some flexibility in the rating system. For instance, in a sermon setting, an idea that includes partner discussions will automatically be labeled as medium risk. However, in a staff meeting or small-group setting, discussion is an expected component of the teaching. So an idea of that type could easily be judged low risk among your pastoral staff or during a board meeting.

In the end, however, all these ratings are subjective. Something our editors have deemed as high risk might actually be a low-risk experience for your congregation, or vice versa. You know your people best, so feel free to ignore our risk rating if it doesn't seem quite right when considering your own church or small group.

About Discussion and Debriefing

As Alan Nelson said in his introduction, "Even a modest time spent reflecting on an activity deepens learning." As learners take time to discuss an experience, they become more active participants in your teaching and deepen their relational connections with other members of the congregation. You'll find that this book doesn't shy away from asking people to think, talk, and react to your teaching.

Still, if your congregation is not used to talking during church, some people may feel reluctant to participate in debriefing activities—and that's OK. Encourage your people to overcome their initial jitters and to give it a try anyway. Most will find the discussion process a valuable—and memorable—experience that helps them engage more deeply with the content of your teaching. And the more you incorporate discussion moments during your sermons and Sunday school lessons, the more your congregation will warm to the experience. They'll even begin to look forward to "their time" within the worship service.

However, if the people in your care are genuinely opposed to talking with others during church, feel free to ask your congregants to quietly reflect on the discussion questions by themselves instead of talking about them with a partner or small group. Again, you know your people best, so feel free to tailor these ideas to fit their personalities and comfort levels.

Remember to Rely on the Holy Spirit to Bring Fruit Out of Your Teaching!

Last but definitely not least, when using an idea from this book, please remember that you aren't alone up there behind the pulpit or in front of a Sunday school class or when leading a pastoral board meeting. God himself is the one who transforms a life, so dedicate yourself to prayer as a natural part of these ideas. Ask God to bless your teaching efforts each time, and then rely on his Holy Spirit to facilitate the active-learning experience and to bring about lasting change in the lives of your listeners. After all, that's what *Make It Stick* is all about—helping you to be the tool that Jesus uses to plant his Word in the lives of others.

PART two

the
experiences

make your message stick...from the pulpit

In this section you'll find 25 creative ideas for interactive sermon illustrations to use during your preaching time. The ideas here vary in style and content, but all conform to the following standards:

- They are drawn from specific Scripture passages and themes.
- They somehow involve everyone in the audience in the learning experience.
- They are appropriate for congregations of just about any size, from 10 to 10,000 people.
- They can be done with few (or no) props and minimal preparation.

As mentioned previously, debriefing and partner discussions are often a part of these interactive illustrations. Remember that if your congregation is not used to talking during church, some people may feel reluctant to participate in this kind of discussion. Encourage your people to overcome their initial jitters and to give it a try anyway—but if all else fails, feel free to ask your congregants to quietly reflect on the discussion questions by themselves instead of talking about them with a partner or small group. Again, you know your people best, so feel free to tailor these ideas to fit their personalities and comfort levels.

You'll notice that Bibles are never listed among the supplies. Please understand that this doesn't mean we expect you to omit Scripture from your teaching; it simply means that we expect Bibles to always be present during your teaching and figured you didn't need us to remind you of that each and every time.

You'll also notice that prayer is always included in your preparation instructions. This doesn't mean we think you might forget to pray about your sermons. It is simply our way of acknowledging—and encouraging you to acknowledge—that God himself is the one who reveals truth through your teaching and through these ideas. And besides, we figure there can never be too much prayer in this world of ours.

1

Pew Expectations

Risk Rating: Low

Scripture: Romans 5:3-4

Key Verse: "We can rejoice, too, when we run into problems and trials" (Romans 5:3a).

Theme: Discomfort

Point: We need not be afraid of experiencing discomfort in life.

Synopsis: Audience members will feel uncomfortable about an unexpected delay in the church service.

Supplies: None

Preparation: Let your pastoral staff know your plans for beginning your sermon, and pray for God to bless your teaching efforts today.

Begin your church's worship service in the customary way. When it's time for you to begin the sermon, simply remain seated as if someone else is supposed to get up and speak. Listen carefully for the sounds of discomfort your silence inspires, such as shuffling papers, murmurs, coughing, nervous laughter, and so on. Wait at least five minutes, or until someone asks about your inactivity.

When you finally stand to speak, pay attention to your congregation's signs of relief such as sighs, smiles, or even applause. Then ask audience members to raise their hands in response to the following questions:

• *How many of you felt uncomfortable with the unexpected delay in our service this morning?*

• *How many of you felt uncomfortable in other situations during the past week?*

• *How many of you just fibbed about not feeling uncomfortable?*

Next, spend a few minutes discussing the mood swings you and your congregation just experienced together. Point out the signs of discomfort you noticed and the signs of relief you spotted after you finally stood up to speak. If you are comfortable doing so, allow audience members to share their feelings during the experience with one another or with the entire congregation. Then say:

> Tip
>
> As you sit in silence during this activity, it's possible that the Holy Spirit will begin to minister individually to those in your congregation. If you sense a move of God's Spirit among your people, be sensitive to his leading and respond accordingly.

*No matter what our expectations, no matter how carefully we plan, no matter what our circumstances, at some point—often at many points in the same day!—we feel uncomfortable about our situations in life. Maybe we're uncomfortable with our relatives or unhappy in our work or stressed about the future or plagued with a disability. But no matter what the situation, **we need not be afraid of experiencing discomfort in life**, and in Romans 5:3-4 the Apostle Paul tells us why.*

Read the words of Romans 5:3-4 to your congregation. Then continue your sermon as planned.

Hands in Your Pockets

Risk Rating: Medium

Scripture: Romans 7:4-6

Key Verse: "Now we can serve God" (Romans 7:6b).

Theme: Freedom

Point: Through the power of Christ and the presence of his Holy Spirit, you've been set free to experience and serve God without limitation!

Synopsis: Audience members will try to pick up a book without using their hands.

Supplies: Hymnals or Bibles placed within reach of audience members

Preparation: Acquire your supplies ahead of time, and pray for God to bless your teaching efforts today.

At the appropriate time during your sermon, instruct everyone to take a moment to stand up and stretch. Tell people to remain standing for the next portion of your talk. Say:

I'd like to try a little experiment now. This may seem a bit unusual, but stay with me. I promise not to embarrass you or to ask you to do anything illegal!

Have those people wearing clothing with pockets form their hands into fists and place them within their pockets. Ask everyone else to close their hands into fists, to cross their arms over their chests, and to place their fists securely under their arms. When everyone's hands are hidden, say:

OK, I'd like to ask you to keep your hands out of commission for the rest of this exercise. Here's what I'd like you to do: Pick up a hymnal [or a Bible]

from the pew [or chair] in front of you. Feel free to work alone or in pairs, but remember, your hands must remain either in your pockets or under your arms at all times.

Let participants spend a few moments trying to pick up a hymnal or Bible without using their hands. Although the overwhelming majority will be unsuccessful at this, you may have one or two creative individuals who are able to overcome their limitation and complete the task. That's OK! The point of this exercise is not to make it impossible for everyone to complete the task, but simply to make it noticeably difficult.

After folks have had time to attempt this feat, tell them they may now free their hands and try again.

Have people return the books to their places and sit down. Say: *Find a friend nearby and describe your reaction to the challenge of picking up a book without using your hands.*

Tip

If the people in your care are genuinely opposed to talking with others during church, then feel free to ask your congregants to quietly reflect on the discussion questions individually instead of talking about them with a partner.

Ask pairs to turn to Romans 7:4-6 in their Bibles and to read along silently as you read the passage aloud. After reading, ask people to reflect on these questions:

• *How was your attempt to pick up a book without using your hands similar to the situation Paul describes in this passage? Explain.*

• *How does a relationship with Jesus free us to really serve God?*

• *What limits you from giving your all to a relationship with Jesus?*

Close this portion of your sermon by saying:

In a very real, spiritual sense, you don't have to live your life with your "hands in your pockets"—limited and handicapped by sin and legalistic expectations. **Through the power of Christ and the presence of his Holy Spirit, you've been set free to experience and serve God without limitation.**

Ready, Set, Pray

Risk Rating: Low

Scripture: Romans 8:22-27

Key Verse: "We don't know what God wants us to pray for" (Romans 8:26b).

Theme: Prayer

Point: God's Spirit is constantly interceding for us when we pray.

Synopsis: Audience members will experience an impromptu prayer time.

Supplies: None

Preparation: Pray for God to bless your teaching efforts today.

At a midpoint in your sermon on Romans 8:22-27, say:

Let's try something that might be a little unexpected right now. Everyone bow your heads, please, as we see if we can experience what Romans 8:22-27 is talking about. When I give the word, start praying about whatever God may bring to mind. Ready? Set? Pray!

Let a few minutes of silence pass as people in your congregation collect their thoughts and begin to pray. Allot as much time for this impromptu prayer as you feel is appropriate, but try to allow at least three or four minutes to pass before interrupting the silence.

When you are ready, call the attention of the congregation back to you. Then ask your audience to individually reflect on these questions:

• *What made it easy or difficult for you to pray "at a moment's notice"? Why do you suppose that was the case?*

• *Did you feel distracted and unable to focus during our prayer time? Why or why not?*

    • *How did you know what to pray about? Or did you have trouble thinking of words to say to God during the silence?*

    • *What weaknesses about prayer did you recognize during our silent time? How did, or might, the Holy Spirit help you overcome those weaknesses?*

Afterward say:

Some of us just experienced our human weaknesses in prayer. We couldn't pray meaningfully for even a few minutes. Others of us had a great time of prayer, despite the rushed and shortened amount of time. Either way, we can take confidence in knowing that **God's Spirit is constantly interceding for us when we pray***.*

Continue your sermon as planned.

Spiritual Gifts Indicators

Risk Rating: Medium

Scripture: Romans 12:6-8

Key Verse: "God has given us different gifts for doing certain things well" (Romans 12:6a).

Theme: Spiritual Gifts

Point: God has given each of us the ability to do certain things well.

Synopsis: Congregants will take a brief spiritual-gifts inventory to help them discover their giftedness.

Supplies: Photocopies of the "Spiritual Gifts Indicator" (pp. 36-37). You'll need enough copies of the indicator for everyone in the congregation to have one. You'll also need pencils or pens.

Preparation: Acquire your supplies ahead of time, and pray for God to bless your teaching efforts today.

Have ushers distribute photocopies of the "Spiritual Gifts Indicator" to each person as he or she enters the auditorium. Be sure to make pencils or pens available to congregation members as well.

At the appropriate time during your sermon on Romans 12:6-8, say:

Today I want to do more than simply talk about some of the spiritual gifts Paul identified in Romans 12:6-8. I'd like to help you explore your possible giftedness in these areas, right here, right now.

Have congregation members take out their copies of the "Spiritual Gifts Indicator" and pencils. Say:

This brief little worksheet will help you discover which gifts you might possess. Take a few minutes right now to complete your worksheet, and then be prepared to talk about your results with a partner when you're done.

Give people five to seven minutes to complete their worksheets. Encourage people to be honest as they complete the questionnaire and to try to identify one or more areas of possible giftedness.

Wrap up this experience by saying:

Romans 12:6-8 makes it clear that **God has given each of us the ability to do certain things well.** *Now that we have some idea of what those things might be, let's commit to helping each other to use those gifts of God in ways that honor him.*

Tip

If the people in your care are genuinely opposed to talking with others during church, then feel free to ask your congregants to quietly reflect on the discussion questions individually instead of talking about them with a partner or small group.

Spiritual Gifts Indicator

This spiritual gifts indicator is based on the gifts listed in Romans 12:6-8. Other spiritual gifts are listed in 1 Corinthians 12:4-11, 27-31; Ephesians 4:7-13; and 1 Peter 4:10-11.

Read each of the following statements and determine how well it describes you. Mark the statements according to the following scale:

M = This describes me **most** of the time.

S = This describes me **sometimes**.

N = This does **not** really describe me.

___ 1. I look for creative ways to meet others' needs.

___ 2. People generally look to me to make the first move.

___ 3. I try hard to help others feel good about themselves.

___ 4. Teaching a Sunday school class or Bible study interests me.

___ 5. I'm likely to mow a neighbor's lawn or take a meal to someone who has been sick.

___ 6. I'm drawn to people others might consider "outcasts."

___ 7. I'm likely to notice when those around me are feeling down.

___ 8. I like the idea of sharing what God has told me with others.

___ 9. Giving is an important part of my financial plan.

___10. I'm likely to generate enthusiasm among others.

___11. When I lend things, I don't worry about getting them back.

___12. Others tell me I explain things in a clear, easy-to-understand way.

___13. I appreciate what others do, and I tell them so.

___14. I feel called to tell others what God reveals to me.

___15. I'm not bothered when my work goes unnoticed.

___16. People who need help solving problems often ask for my opinion.

___17. I think everyone deserves second and third chances.

___18. I enjoy preparing lessons because I like sharing what I learn with others.

___19. I'm interested in ministering to prisoners, the homeless, the disabled, and people in similar situations.

___20. People tell me I present biblical messages in a clear, compelling way.

___21. I'm likely to volunteer for tasks others may have neglected.

Each statement describes a possible demonstration of one of the spiritual gifts listed in Romans 12:6-8. Statements you marked with an **M** could indicate giftedness in the corresponding spiritual gift. Two or more related statements marked with an **S** could also indicate giftedness.

Match your responses with the gifts below by circling the statement numbers that you ranked with an **M**. Those qualities with the most **M** rankings or multiple **S** rankings are probably your spiritual gifts.

- prophecy: 8, 14, 20
- serving: 5, 15, 21
- teaching: 4, 12, 18
- showing mercy: 6, 17, 19
- encouraging: 3, 7, 13
- giving: 1, 9, 11
- leading: 2, 10, 16

5

Crisp Clap

Risk Rating: Low

Scripture: Romans 15:5-7

Key Verse: "All of you can join together with one voice" (Romans 15:6a).

Theme: Unity

Point: A unified church body is a powerful church body.

Synopsis: Audience members will try to clap in unison.

Supplies: None

Preparation: Pray for God to bless your teaching efforts today.

After teaching a bit about unity as described in Romans 15:5-7, say:

*Romans 15:5-7 is a powerful challenge for our church and for the church at large. **A unified church body is a powerful church body.** However, we often talk about unity but rarely get a glimpse of what that looks or sounds like. Let's try a little exercise right now to see if we can glimpse unity in action.*

Ask participants to put down anything they may be holding in their hands. Then tell them you're going to demonstrate something for them to do in a moment, and ask them to pay close attention to you during this demonstration. Lift your hands above your head with your palms facing each other. Then count: *One, two, clap!* On the word *clap*, bring your hands together to make a loud clapping sound.

Ask your congregation to stand. Say:

Now let's all try this activity together. When I give the count, let's see if we can all clap at exactly the same time. Ready? One, two, clap!

Hopefully, you all will hear one solid, unified clap that fills your auditorium—but there may be a few clappers who slap their palms too soon or too late. If that happens, that's OK—just repeat the exercise a few times until you get at least one completely unified clap. (And if you like that sound, feel free to repeat it more than once!) It's amazing how singular this clap can sound if everyone in your audience closely follows your directions.

After your congregation has performed at least one unified clap, have participants give their neighbors a high five for their efforts, and then have everyone return to their seats.

Continue your sermon as planned, discussing how, if we all are determined to work together, our unity can make an impressive impact on anyone who sees or hears us.

Can You Read My Mind?

Risk Rating: Low

Scripture: 1 Corinthians 2:10-16

Key Verse: "We have the mind of Christ"
(1 Corinthians 2:16b).

Theme: God's Will

Point: With God's Holy Spirit helping us, we can discover God's will as it's revealed through the pages of the Bible.

Synopsis: Audience members will attempt to "read" minds.

Supplies: None

Preparation: Pray for God to bless your teaching efforts today.

At the appropriate time during your sermon, ask everyone in the audience to stand. Say:

We're going to try an exercise now to see if any of you can read my mind!

If you are comfortable hamming things up a bit, tell your congregation that you've been practicing a broadband broadcast of your thoughts lately and—after a few interesting mishaps—you think you've finally gotten it down. Now you are simply looking for a few good men and women who can receive that broadcast and read your mind. Feel free to embellish this silly story as much as you wish.

When you're ready, tell people that you've chosen a number between 1 and 10, and now you'd like them to tell you which number you've chosen. Let your selection be the number 9, but don't tell anyone that. Allow a moment or two for people to make their choices. Then instruct anyone who chose the number 1 to sit down. Next, instruct anyone who chose the number 2 to sit down. Continue having group members sit down (be sure to include those who chose the number 10 in a group of people selected to sit down) until only the people who chose the number 9 are left standing. Congratulate these people profusely, and have the rest of the audience give them a round of applause. Play up the fact that these people have apparently received your thought broadcast perfectly and have actually read your mind. Then instruct the remaining people to be seated.

Pause for a moment, and then scratch your head and suggest that there might be one other possibility to consider. It might be that no one *really* read your mind, that everyone only took a guess at what they hoped you were thinking, and that some of them simply guessed correctly. Ask group members to raise their hands if that was the case with them. Then shake your head mournfully, promise to practice thought broadcasting more in the future, and say:

> **Tip**
>
> It's possible that no one will be left standing when you reveal that you selected the number 9—and that's OK. In this situation, simply lament the fact that no one could receive your thought broadcast and highlight that everyone was apparently just guessing at what they hoped you were thinking.

Unfortunately, most of us approach the idea of discovering God's will with the same kind of random guessing that we used during this fake mind-reading exercise. But Scripture tells us that we don't have to live our relationship with Jesus in this way.

Read aloud 1 Corinthians 2:10-16, with an emphasis on verses 10 and 16. Say:

With God's Holy Spirit helping us, we can discover God's will as it's revealed through the pages of the Bible. *Let's explore more about what that means during the rest of our time together.*

Continue your sermon as planned.

What Is It?

Risk Rating: Low

Scripture: 2 Corinthians 4:17-18

Key Verse: "We fix our gaze on things that cannot be seen" (2 Corinthians 4:18b).

Theme: Perspective

Point: God sees our lives with his unlimited perspective.

Synopsis: Audience members will attempt to identify a figure without a proper sense of perspective.

Supplies: Enough photocopies of the "What Is It?" handout (p. 44) for everyone to have one and pencils or pens

Preparation: Acquire your supplies ahead of time, and pray for God to bless your teaching efforts today.

At the beginning of your sermon have ushers distribute copies of the "What Is It?" handout (p. 44) to everyone in the congregation. When each person has a copy of the circle drawing, say:

The drawing on your handout is an enlarged view of a piece of a larger structure. Please take a moment to identify the structure and indicate where this piece fits on that structure. Feel free to work on this task with a partner or a small group, if you like. Write your ideas right on your handout. You have two minutes. Go.

Call time after two minutes. If your congregation is comfortable with this kind of interaction, ask for volunteers to share their best guesses as to what the drawing actually is. It's very unlikely that anyone will correctly identify the drawing. After a few incorrect guesses, say:

The drawing on your handout is a replica of the fourth rivet on the sixth

secondary support crossbeam located on the west side of the Eiffel Tower in Paris, exactly 120.32 feet from the ground.

Next, ask congregation members to reflect on these questions:

• *Why do you suppose it was nearly impossible to identify exactly what was drawn on the handout?*

• *How was this experience like trying to figure out what God is doing in your life by examining a single action or event?*

Say:

If you've ever seen the Eiffel Tower, you know that while it's beautiful overall, it's not so attractive when you get up close and examine its individual parts. Like our rivet here, individual pieces on a soaring structure appear plain or awkwardly shaped.

> **Tip**
>
> If your congregation is comfortable with it, have audience members find a friend and discuss their responses to the debriefing questions in pairs or small groups.

Our lives are often like that. We will stare closely at a problem or difficult situation and pass judgment on it. Our perspective is limited to our own experience. However, **God sees our lives with his unlimited perspective.** *He sees how every hardship we face contributes to the soaring artwork that he is creating in our lives, and how this present problem is molding us into the glorious architecture of heaven. Let me show you what I mean.*

Read aloud 2 Corinthians 4:17-18, and then continue your sermon as planned. Encourage your congregation to take notes on the rest of your sermon on the back of their handouts and then to take those handouts home as a reminder of the day's teaching.

What Is It?

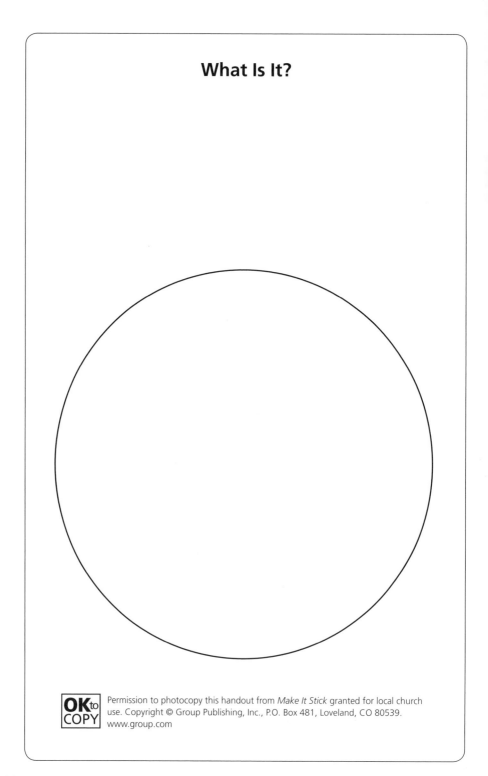

Hidden Strength

Risk Rating: Low

Scripture: 2 Corinthians 12:7-10

Key Verse: "When I am weak, then I am strong" (2 Corinthians 12:10b).

Theme: Weakness

Point: By God's grace, we can be strong in the midst of any weakness.

Synopsis: Audience members will view a clip from the biopic *Ray*.

Supplies: A DVD version of the 2004 film *Ray* (rated PG-13) and the ability to show a clip from this DVD to the congregation

Preparation: Acquire your supplies ahead of time, and pray for God to bless your teaching efforts today. The film clip for this experience is located within track 13 on the DVD, beginning about one hour and nine minutes from the start of the movie. This specific clip runs from time counter point 1:09:27 through 1:12:03. Please be sure to preview this clip to make sure its content is appropriate for your congregation.

Preface this portion of your sermon by telling your congregation the following story:

Most of you have probably heard of the world-famous musician, Ray Charles. When he was a boy, his vision slowly diminished until he was completely blind. During that time he struggled with losing his sight, and his mother struggled with helping him overcome that loss. The film Ray*—a*

dramatization of Ray Charles' life—reveals one particularly compelling moment for both Ray and his mother. Let's watch that scene right now.

Tip

In general, federal copyright laws do not allow you to use videos or DVDs (even ones you own) for any purpose other than home viewing. Though some exceptions allow for the use of short segments of copyrighted material for educational purposes, it's best to be on the safe side. Your church can obtain a license from Christian Video Licensing for a small fee. Just visit www.cvli .org or call 1-888-771-2854 for more information. When using a movie that is not covered by the license, we recommend directly contacting the movie studio to seek permission to use the clip.

Play the clip from the DVD. This scene shows a young Ray Charles running care-free into his family's small house. Because he is nearly blind, he falls and hurts himself near the doorway. He tearfully calls out for his mother. Although the mother stands only a few feet away, she resists the urge to come to his rescue. Instead, she stands silently nearby, forcing the child to cope with the situation himself. After a moment, young Ray stops crying and is surprised to discover that although his sight is nearly gone, his other senses have sharpened as his body compensates for his weakness. He listens intently and hears the sounds of the world around him until at last he recognizes the sound of his mother breathing nearby. And he learns that even in his weakness, he is strong enough to deal with life's hurts.

After showing the clip, ask congregation members to reflect on these questions:

• *What emotions did you have while watching this film clip?*

• *What thoughts went through your mind as you saw young Ray Charles learning to cope with his weakness?*

Next, have congregants open their Bibles to 2 Corinthians 12:7-10. Encourage them to read along silently as you read this passage aloud. After reading, have people in the congregation reflect on these questions:

Tip

If your congregation is comfortable with it, have audience members find a friend and discuss their responses to the debriefing questions in pairs or small groups.

• *Why do you suppose God allows us to feel weak and to suffer in this life?*

• *How would you explain the Apostle Paul's idea that "when we are weak, then we are strong"?*

• *What can you learn from Ray Charles and from the Apostle Paul to help you triumph when you feel weak in the coming days?*

Wrap up this portion of your sermon by saying:

*Life hurts, and when it does we often feel like blind children who've been abandoned by God. But, like Ray Charles and the Apostle Paul, we must remember that we are never alone and that, **by God's grace, we can be strong in the midst of any weakness.***

Lift

Risk Rating: Medium

Scripture: 2 Corinthians 13:3-4

Key Verse: "We, too, are weak, just as Christ was, but…we will be alive with him and will have God's power" (2 Corinthians 13:4b).

Theme: Strength

Point: Our only real strength is found in Christ.

Synopsis: Congregants will attempt to hold their arms in the air for an extended period of time.

Supplies: None

Preparation: Pray for God to bless your teaching efforts today.

At the appropriate time during your sermon, have everyone in the congregation stand up. Instruct participants to stretch out their left arm in front of them and hold that arm at shoulder level. Then instruct audience members to also raise their right arm behind them and to hold that arm at shoulder level. Warn folks to be careful not to poke anybody in the eye as they are stretching out their arms! At this point each person should be holding one arm straight out in front and one arm straight out in back, both at shoulder level. (Yes, this will look pretty funny from your perspective; if your congregation has a sense of humor, threaten to take a picture and use it for blackmail purposes sometime in the future.)

Tell congregation members that you'd like them to simply stay in that position, with their arms outstretched, for as long as they are comfortable. Let them know that when they begin to feel tired or weakened, they are free to lower their arms and sit down. Then continue with your sermon. You might want to tell a story at this point or do some other segment that will last about five minutes or so. Of course, most people in your congregation will be a little distracted during this exercise, so be prepared for that.

Pay attention to the rate at which people finally give up, lower their arms, and sit down. When most of them have lowered their arms and returned to their seats, tell the last few holdouts to also sit down. Then say:

The reason I wanted you to stand with your arms outstretched today was to bring home—in a physical, immediate sense—the truth that the Apostle Paul wrote about in 2 Corinthians 13:3-4.

Read aloud this Bible passage, with special emphasis on the last half of verse 4. Then say: **Our only real strength for life is found in Christ.** *As Paul has said, "We, too, are weak, just as Christ was, but...we will be alive with him and will have God's power."*

Continue your sermon as planned.

10

Liar Liar

Risk Rating: Medium

Scripture: 2 Corinthians 13:8

Key Verse: "For we cannot oppose the truth" (2 Corinthians 13:8a).

Theme: Truth

Point: Our responsibility is to never oppose the truth.

Synopsis: Audience members will view a clip from the film *Liar Liar* and then discuss it in pairs.

Supplies: A DVD version of the 1997 film *Liar Liar* (rated PG-13, starring Jim Carrey) and the ability to show a clip from this DVD to the congregation

Preparation: Acquire your supplies ahead of time, and pray for God to bless your teaching efforts today. The film clip for this experience is located at the beginning of track 8 on the DVD, about 38 minutes from the start of the movie. This specific clip runs from time counter point 0:38:15 through 0:41:57 (the end of track 8). Please be sure to preview this clip to make sure its content is appropriate for your congregation.

Tip

An alternate—and laugh-out-loud, slapstick-funny—clip to use for this illustration is found at the beginning of track 6 in *Liar Liar*, about 26 minutes from the start of the movie. This specific clip runs from time counter point 0:26:35 through 0:28:58. It shows Jim Carrey deliberately trying to tell a lie—and being hilariously thwarted by his own body. One warning though: You'll want to be sure to stop this clip at exactly the 0:28:58 mark, as the actor utters an inappropriate profanity just seconds later. If you use this clip, it'll be best to practice the quick shutoff before presenting it to your congregation.

At the appropriate time during your sermon, read aloud

2 Corinthians 13:8 to your congregation. Say:

*Scripture makes it clear that **our responsibility is to never oppose the truth**. However, that perspective is often distorted and dismissed by our society. A hilarious example of that kind of distortion is found in a scene from the popular Jim Carrey movie* Liar Liar. *In this film, Carrey plays a lawyer whose young son wishes that his dad would always have to tell the truth—no matter what. The wish comes true, and the result is disastrous for the dad. When Carrey finds out what has happened, he tries to convince his son to take back the wish. Let's eavesdrop now and see what happens next.*

Play the clip from the DVD.

Afterward, ask congregation members to find a partner and discuss these questions:

• *What do you think is true and what do you think is false in regard to the perspective on honesty Jim Carrey's character presents?*

• *Is it possible to be truthful without being offensive? Explain.*

• *What do you think it really means when 2 Corinthians 13:8 says we must never oppose the truth?*

• *How might 2 Corinthians 13:8 be applied to Jim Carrey's character and situation in* Liar Liar?

If your congregation is comfortable with dialogue during a sermon, ask several volunteers to share insights gained from their discussion. If not, continue your sermon as planned, offering your own insights in response to the questions.

Tip

In general, federal copyright laws do not allow you to use videos or DVDs (even ones you own) for any purpose other than home viewing. Though some exceptions allow for the use of short segments of copyrighted material for educational purposes, it's best to be on the safe side. Your church can obtain a license from Christian Video Licensing for a small fee. Just visit www.cvli .org or call 1-888-771-2854 for more information. When using a movie that is not covered by the license, we recommend directly contacting the movie studio to seek permission to use the clip.

Tip

If the people in your care are genuinely opposed to talking with others during church, then feel free to ask your congregants to quietly reflect on the discussion questions individually instead of talking about them with a partner or small group.

11

Interesting Impressions

Risk Rating: Medium

Scripture: Galatians 1:13-24

Key Verse: "They praised God because of me" (Galatians 1:24).

Theme: Sharing Faith

Point: We all have a story worth sharing—the story of how God's love has left an impression on our lives.

Synopsis: Audience members will see their own impressions in a sheet of foil.

Supplies: One piece of foil (approximately 6x6 inches) for each person

Preparation: Acquire your supplies ahead of time, and pray for God to bless your teaching efforts today.

Have ushers distribute one piece of foil to each person as he or she enters the auditorium. Have ushers tell congregation members to keep their foil sheets flat until the time comes to use them during the church service.

At the appropriate time during your sermon, ask congregation members to take out their flattened sheets of foil. Say:

Other than the fact that it is shiny, the piece of foil you hold in your hands is pretty bland and uninteresting. Let's do something about that.

Carefully press a foil sheet against your face until it takes on the rough shape of your features. Then instruct congregants to do the same with their foil sheets, leaving their own facial impressions on the foil. Encourage people to show their sculptures to one another. You might even want to hold up a few for everyone to see (with the permission of the owners, of course).

Afterward, say:

A moment ago, all we had were bland, uninteresting pieces of foil. But now that these foil sheets hold impressions of you, they all have a "before and after" story, and suddenly they are all worth talking about.

I wanted us to do this little activity because I think it's a great picture of our approach to sharing our faith. You see, often we feel at a loss for what to say when the opportunity arises to tell someone else about Jesus. We feel just like a bland, flat piece of foil. When that happens, we need to remember that **we all have a story worth sharing—the story of how God's love has left an impression on our lives.** *The Apostle Paul knew this—and he talked about it often. Listen to how he used his own story to tell the people of Galatia about faith in Christ.*

Read aloud Galatians 1:13-24, and then continue your sermon as planned.

IDEA 12

Instant Service

Risk Rating: High

Scripture: Galatians 5:13

Key Verse: "Serve one another in love" (Galatians 5:13b).

Theme: Serving

Point: Serving others is a risky—but rewarding—business.

Synopsis: Audience members will engage in impromptu acts of service.

Supplies: None

Preparation: Pray for God to bless your teaching efforts today.

Begin this portion of your sermon by reading aloud Galatians 5:13, with emphasis on the last half of the verse, "serve one another in love." Then tell your people that you want to do more than simply talk about this verse today; you want to provide an opportunity for people to put the Scripture into action.

Say: *At this point during our service, I'm going to ask you to step out of your comfort zone just a bit. I know this will feel like a stretch for some of you, but you can take heart in knowing that this activity has been done numerous times with audiences as large as several hundred people—and not once has anyone ever been maimed or killed during the experience!*

Have members of your congregation form service teams of three (or four, if necessary). Have each team member number off from 1 to 3 (it's OK if two people have the same number within a group of four). Tell congregation members they'll take turns sending the other members of their service teams on "instant service projects" that must meet the following guidelines. Read these guidelines aloud and clearly so everyone understands:

• *A project must serve at least one other member of the congregation.*

• *A project must include a word or action designed to encourage, such as a sincere compliment, a 30-second shoulder rub, a round of applause, a hug, and so on.*

• *A project must be able to be completed in 30 seconds or less.*

• *No project can make the person doing it feel terribly uncomfortable. If you're too uneasy about a particular project, ask for another option. However, don't let a little discomfort disable you from service. Remember, service sometimes stretches us beyond our comfortable boundaries.*

> **Tip**
>
> If you have the capability to project the "instant service project" guidelines on a PowerPoint display or overhead transparency that everyone can refer to during this activity, that will help your congregation feel more confident in doing this exercise.

When everyone is ready, instruct groups to make the Ones the first team members to be in charge. Tell the Ones they have 15 seconds (or so) to give each of their team members a specific service project to accomplish. For instance, they may send Two off to compliment someone's dress and Three to thank a pastor for his or her dedication to the church. Or they might send Two and Three off together to applaud people who volunteer in the church's worship ministry or to say a happy thank you to the sound engineers. Encourage teams to be creative and enthusiastic.

Then say: *Ready? Go serve!*

Call time after 30 seconds and have everyone return to his or her original team. Then repeat the process, this time designating the twos as the people in charge of the teams. Repeat one last time, with the threes acting as the people in charge.

Afterward, have people return to their seats. Say:

*As we can see from our experience today, **serving others is a risky—but rewarding—business.** As Galatians 5:13 reveals, Christ has set us free to serve one another in love. Let's explore more about what that means.*

Continue your sermon as planned.

13

Wiped Clean

Risk Rating: Low

Scripture: Ephesians 1:4-7

Key Verse: "He purchased our freedom with the blood of his Son" (Ephesians1:7b).

Theme: Forgiveness

Point: Because of Christ's sacrifice, we have been forgiven, and our sins have been wiped away.

Synopsis: Congregants will see a permanent mark unexpectedly erased from sight.

Supplies: A dry-erase whiteboard, a dark *permanent* marker (it's best to avoid using a black marker because of possible racial misinterpretation of the color), a red *dry erase* marker, and an eraser for the whiteboard

Preparation: Acquire your supplies ahead of time, and pray for God to bless your teaching efforts today. You might also want to practice this illustration ahead of time to make sure the markers you are using are compatible with the instructions. Before your sermon, set up the dry erase whiteboard at the front of the auditorium, and place your markers and eraser nearby.

Use this idea to really bring home the message of Ephesians 1:4-7, that Jesus' blood sacrifice on the cross has provided the way for our sins to be forgiven.

After speaking for a bit on the content of Ephesians 1:4-7, tell the congregation that you want to show them a new way to think about the truth that Jesus' blood can forgive our sins. Hold up the dark permanent marker and say:

This permanent marker represents sin. Because it leaves a permanent mark, it's not supposed to be used on a whiteboard like this one.

Ask a volunteer to join you, and have that individual confirm that the marker is indeed a permanent one. Next, ask the volunteer to write "SIN" in big, bold, capital letters on the whiteboard. When he or she is finished, thank your volunteer and ask that person to return to the audience. Say:

We've all sinned, and as far as we're concerned, that sin has left a big, indelible mark on our souls.

Call up another volunteer and ask that person to use the eraser to try and remove the "SIN" mark from the whiteboard. After that person demonstrates that the permanent ink can't be erased from the board, dismiss him or her. Then say:

We have no way to erase the permanent mark of sin from our lives. And that sin separates us from God. However, in his great love and compassion, God sent Jesus to die on the cross, bearing our sins.

Hold up the red marker and say: *This red marker will represent Jesus' blood that covers our sins.*

Invite a third volunteer to the front. Have that person use the red dry erase marker to quickly, and *completely*, cover every trace of the word "SIN" on the whiteboard. Then dismiss that volunteer and say:

Since the blood of Jesus' sacrifice covers our sins, we can seek God's forgiveness in our lives. When we do that, he wipes clean the sin from our souls and restores us to an intimate relationship with him.

Call forward one last volunteer. Ask that person to erase the entire board. This time, the eraser will remove everything from the board, including both the red ink and the dark permanent ink. Dismiss the last volunteer and reread Ephesians 1:4-7, with emphasis on verse 7. Then motion to the whiteboard and say:

Because of Christ's sacrifice, we have been forgiven, and our sins have been wiped away.

Continue your sermon as planned.

14

A Squiggle in Eternity

Risk Rating: Low

Scripture: Ephesians 4:4-8

Key Verse: "He has given each one of us a special gift" (Ephesians 4:7a).

Theme: Body of Christ

Point: When we use our gifts in relationship with each other, we bring about unexpected and exciting developments in God's great design.

Synopsis: Volunteers from the congregation will each contribute a small part to an overall design.

Supplies: An overhead projector and screen, a blank transparency, and a transparency pen

Preparation: Acquire your supplies ahead of time, and pray for God to bless your teaching efforts today.

Set up an overhead projector and screen near the pulpit. At the appropriate time during your sermon, call attention to the projector, and then draw a free-form squiggle on a blank transparency. Position the transparency so everyone can see what's on it. Say:

This fancy little squiggle here is just the beginning of a grand design. Take a moment now to imagine what you think the final design will look like.

Next, designate five distinct teams within your congregation, and select one volunteer from each team to be its leader. Tell your volunteers you'd like each of them to add one detail to the squiggle that will transform it into what they imagine it will be in the end. Let them know they may add anything that helps to bring meaning to the developing picture.

Have leaders take turns soliciting advice from their teams and then adding new designs to the transparency. Encourage the last leader to somehow tie up all the squiggles into a distinctive, finished overall design.

Afterward, present the finished design to the congregation and encourage listeners to consider these questions:

• *How does the final picture compare to what you initially imagined when you saw the squiggle?*

• *What changed your perspective?*

Read aloud Ephesians 4:4-8; then ask your audience to consider this question: *How is this picture like what happens in the body of Christ as each person makes a contribution to God's overall design?*

Say: *God has given each of us a special gift, and **when we use our gifts in relationship with each other, we bring about unexpected and exciting developments in God's great design** for our world.*

15

"I Don't Think You're a Pig"

Risk Rating: Medium

Scripture: Ephesians 4:29

Key Verse: "Let everything you say be good and helpful" (Ephesians 4:29b).

Theme: Encouragement

Point: Let's remember to encourage others with what we say—and *how* we say it.

Synopsis: Audience members will conduct an experiment in communication.

Supplies: A PowerPoint slide or transparency with the sentence "I don't think you're a pig" written clearly upon it, and the ability to project that sentence so that everyone in the congregation can read it

Preparation: Acquire your supplies ahead of time, and pray for God to bless your teaching efforts today.

Begin this activity by reading aloud Ephesians 4:29b:

"Let everything you say be good and helpful, so that your words will be an encouragement to those who hear them."

Then say:

Can you imagine how our church would change if all of us followed the Apostle Paul's advice in this Scripture? That, I think, would be a wonderful experience for all of us—and it gives us a great goal to pursue. However, it's important for us to realize that this passage of Scripture encompasses more than just what we say, but also how we say it. Let me demonstrate.

Show your congregation the sentence "I don't think you're a pig."

Say: *When you first read this sentence, it seems to mean only one thing.*

But see how the meaning of the sentence changes when you emphasize differ-ent words as you say it.

Ask everyone who was born in January or February to stand. Tell these people that you'd like them to shout out the sentence for the rest of the congregation, putting emphasis on the first word:

"*I* don't think you're a pig."

Allow these group members to be seated, and then say:

What these people just said was pretty straightforward. But the implied meaning was completely different. By emphasizing the first word of this sentence, they've communi-cated something like this: "I don't think you're a pig, but everyone else does!"

Have other group members take turns shouting out the sentence, putting empha-sis on a different word each time. For example, everyone born in March and April might read the sentence with an emphasis on the second word; everyone born in May and June would read with an emphasis on the third word; and so on. After each reading, take a moment to point out how the sentence could be under-stood—or misunderstood. For instance:

> **Tip**
>
> If the people in your care are genuinely opposed to talking with others during church, then feel free to ask your congregants to quietly reflect on the discussion questions individually instead of talking about them with a partner or small group.

• Emphasizing the second word, "DON'T," communicates that the speaker really doesn't think you are a pig.

• Emphasizing the third word, "THINK," communicates something like, "I don't THINK you're a pig—I KNOW you are!"

• Emphasizing the fourth word, "YOU'RE," communicates some-thing like, "I don't think YOU'RE a pig—but your friends sure are!"

• Emphasizing the fifth word, "A," communicates something like, "I don't think you're A pig—I think you're a whole stinky pigpen full of them!"

• Emphasizing the last word, "PIG," communicates something like, "I don't think you're a PIG—but you are some other kind of smelly animal!"

After this exercise, have everyone find a friend nearby to discuss these questions:

• *Why do you suppose it's so easy for us to insult each other with our words?*

• *What keeps us from truly letting everything we say be good and helpful for each other?*

• *What can we learn from today's little exercise to help us more fully follow Paul's advice in Ephesians 4:29 this week?*

Say: *Ephesians 4:29 makes it clear that words we speak to each other are important.* **Let's remember to encourage others with what we say—and how we say it.**

Penny for Your Future

Risk Rating: Medium

Scripture: Philippians 1:12-14

Key Verse: "Everything that has happened to me here has helped to spread the Good News" (Philippians 1:12b).

Theme: The Future

Point: No matter what the future holds, we can gain confidence in knowing that God is active in both the good times and the hard times we face.

Synopsis: Audience members will try to predict the future based on coin tosses.

Supplies: Enough pennies for each person in your congregation to have one, as well as paper and pencils

Preparation: Acquire your supplies ahead of time, and pray for God to bless your teaching efforts today.

Have ushers distribute paper, a pencil, and one penny to each person in your congregation. Have each person draw two columns on his or her paper, labeling one column as "Good Times" and the other as "Hard Times." Then say:

Right now I want you to try to predict your future using an extremely scientific method: with the flip of a coin! Let heads represent good times and tails represent hard times. With this high-tech system, you can find out exactly what percentage of your future will be spent experiencing pleasure and what percentage will be spent enduring hard times.

Have audience members quickly execute 10 coin tosses with their pennies, marking the appropriate column on their papers each time.

When they have 10 marks on their papers, have people find a partner to compare what their future holds, according to the less-than-accurate indicator of coin tosses. Then have partners explore answers to these questions:

Tip

If the people in your care are genuinely opposed to talking with others during church, then feel free to ask your congregants to quietly reflect on the discussion questions individually instead of talking about them with a partner or small group.

• *What do you hope your future really holds?*

• *Why do you suppose God will allow both good times and hard times to fill your future?*

• *What do you think is the best way to view both good times and hard times in life? Explain.*

Say: **No matter what the future holds, we can gain confidence in knowing that God is active in both the good times and the hard times we face.** *The Apostle Paul learned this truth thousands of years ago, even when he was imprisoned for simply preaching about Jesus Christ. Listen to what he said about that situation.*

Read aloud Philippians 1:12-14; then continue with your sermon as planned.

Scripture Mirrors

Risk Rating: Medium

Scripture: Philippians 2:5-11

Key Verse: "You must have the same attitude that Christ Jesus had" (Philippians 2:5).

Theme: Humility

Point: We are best served in this life when we mirror the humble attitude that Christ displayed.

Synopsis: Audience members will mimic a pantomimed expression of Philippians 2:5-11.

Supplies: Three copies of the "Scripture Mirrors" handout (p. 67) and two volunteers to help you lead the experience

Preparation: Acquire your supplies ahead of time, and recruit two volunteers to help lead the creative pantomime of this exercise. Pray for God to bless your teaching efforts today.

A week or so before your sermon, ask creative members of your congregation to practice the worship pantomime indicated on the "Scripture Mirrors" handout (p. 67). Make sure each volunteer gets a copy of the handout, but tell your performers that they can perform the pantomime as it is written or (if they are so inclined) they can tailor it as needed to better fit the personality of your congregation. Also, be sure to let your performers know that they won't be speaking; they will be acting out their motions as you read aloud the Scripture passage.

At the appropriate time during your sermon, say:

We are best served in this life when we mirror the humble attitude

that Christ displayed. *As a physical reminder of that truth, I'd like to read a passage of Scripture from Philippians that describes beautifully the humility of Jesus. As I read, two volunteers will visually represent the words of the passage.*

Call your volunteers forward; then read Philippians 2:5-11 aloud while they act out the accompanying motions. Then say:

Now I'd like everyone to stand as I repeat this reading. This time, I'd like you to join in the visual representation of the verses. Watch our volunteers and simply mirror their motions right where you are standing. Ready? Let's begin.

Read Philippians 2:5-11 again, pausing as needed to allow everyone to perform the appropriate motions. Afterward, have everyone return to his or her seat and continue your sermon as planned.

> ## Tip
>
> When the congregation acts out the pantomime in response to Philippians 2:5-11, you may find a sense of worship and awe takes over the auditorium. Be sensitive to that possibility, and consider spending a moment in silence or in prayer at the conclusion of this activity if it feels appropriate.

Scripture Mirrors

- You must have the same attitude that Christ Jesus had *(stand with hands clasped and head down)*.

- Though he was God *(lift head and look outward, sweeping hands out across the horizon, as though performing an act of creation)*,

- he did not think of equality with God as something to cling to. Instead, he gave up his divine privileges *(quickly kneel, bow head, and cover head with crossed arms)*;

- he took the humble position of a slave and was born as a human being *(extend hands, cupping them together as though offering service)*.

- When he appeared in human form *(look at arms in astonishment as though for the first time)*,

- he humbled himself in obedience to God and died a criminal's death on a cross. *(While still kneeling, extend arms out as though nailed to a cross, and bow head.)*

- Therefore, God elevated him to the place of highest honor *(with arms still extended, stand and look up)*

- and gave him the name above all other names *(raise arms toward heaven)*,

- that at the name of Jesus every knee should bow, in heaven *(quickly bring arms down; then raise them toward heaven again)*

- and on earth *(extend arms toward the audience)*

- and under the earth *(spread arms downward toward the floor)*,

- and every tongue confess that Jesus Christ is Lord *(kneel)*,

- to the glory of God the Father. *(Raise arms and lift face toward heaven, smiling.)*

IDEA 18

10-Second Masterpiece

Risk Rating: Low

Scripture: Colossians 1:11-12

Key Verse: "You will be strengthened with all his glorious power so you will have all the endurance and patience you need" (Colossians 1:11b).

Theme: Patience

Point: God is creating a masterpiece in you, so don't rush him.

Synopsis: Audience members will try to create an artistic masterpiece in only 10 seconds.

Supplies: Paper, pencils, a stool, and a volunteer

Preparation: Acquire your supplies ahead of time, and arrange for a volunteer to help you with this activity. Also, pray for God to bless your teaching efforts today.

When people enter your church's auditorium, have ushers give each person a sheet of paper and a pencil. Have the ushers explain that people will need these later during your sermon.

At the appropriate time during your sermon, tell people to take out their paper and pencils. Place a stool up front, near the pulpit, and call for your volunteer to come up and sit on the stool. Say:

My volunteer here has agreed to be a model for today's sermon. Your task is to create a masterpiece-quality pencil drawing of our model. As you can see, our original is a wonderful example of God's creation. With a fine model like this, you should be able to draw your masterpiece in no time at all. Everyone ready? OK, go!

Once participants have begun to draw, silently count off 10 seconds;

then abruptly tell them their time is up. Send ushers to collect drawings from everyone, and have them brought to you.

Begin thumbing through the drawings. Act disappointed and slightly offended by the poor quality of so many barely-begun drawings. Play this up as much as you feel comfortable doing. Then ask your people to raise their hands in response to this question:

> • *How many of you think it was unfair of me to expect you to produce a masterpiece in only 10 seconds?*

Acknowledge the hands, and then say:

> *It takes time, patience, and endurance for a true artist to create an authentic masterpiece. Yet many of us treat God as though he should complete his work of art in our spiritual, emotional, and physical lives right now, in 10 seconds or less! But that's not the way God works. Listen to what the Scripture says.*

Read aloud Colossians 1:11-12. Say:

> **God is creating a masterpiece in you, so don't rush him!** *Let his Spirit and power strengthen you so that you will have all the patience and endurance you need to live out your life as God's evermore-beautiful work of art.*

Then continue your sermon as planned.

Tip

Some people will try to keep drawing even after you've announced that time is up. Feel free to good-naturedly badger these folks into laying down their pencils and turning in their drawings without allowing them to finish.

In-Your-Face Prayer

Risk Rating: High

Scripture: 1 Thessalonians 1:2-3

Key Verse: "We…pray for you constantly"
(1 Thessalonians 1:2).

Theme: Praying for Others

Point: We can follow the Apostle Paul's example
when praying for others.

Synopsis: Audience members will pray for others in
a socially uncomfortable situation.

Supplies: None

Preparation: Pray for God to bless your teaching
efforts today.

Say: *Today I am going to ask you to stretch a little bit, and
some of you are going to feel a little uncomfortable with this activity. But I
promise not to embarrass anybody—and I promise that if you participate
fully, you will be glad you did.*

Have everyone stand and find a partner nearby. Have partners face
each other. Say:

*For the next 90 seconds, look your partner in the eye and, without speak-
ing a word aloud, pray for that person as best you can. Try hard not to break
eye contact during the full 90 seconds. Ready? Begin.*

When time expires, thank everyone, and have partners return to their
seats and discuss these questions with someone sitting nearby:

• *What emotions did you feel while you were forced to stare into another's
eyes as you prayed?*

• *On a scale of 1 to 10, how would you rate your comfort level with this activity? Consider 1 as very uncomfortable and 10 as completely comfortable. Explain your answer.*

• *How was this experience like or unlike your normal experience of praying for others?*

Say: *Often when praying for others we feel the pressure and discomfort that many of us felt during this exercise. We don't know what to pray or how to pray or why to pray, and that sometimes can prevent us from praying at all. When we face those situations in the future,* **we can follow the Apostle Paul's example when praying for others.** *Let's look at that example in Scripture right now, in 1 Thessalonians 1:2-3.*

Read aloud the Bible passage, and then continue your sermon as planned.

20

Letters From God

Risk Rating: Low

Scripture: 1 Thessalonians 5:9-11

Key Verse: "For God chose to save us through our Lord Jesus Christ" (1 Thessalonians 5:9a).

Theme: Salvation

Point: Remember with joy the good news that Jesus saves!

Synopsis: Audience members will paraphrase Scripture as a means of encouraging themselves in the coming week.

Supplies: Enough index cards, pencils, and envelopes for each person to have one of each. You'll also need postage stamps.

Preparation: Acquire your supplies ahead of time, and pray for God to bless your teaching efforts today.

When people enter your church's auditorium, have ushers give each person an index card, a pencil, and an envelope. Have the ushers explain that people will need these later.

At the appropriate time during your sermon, say:

I have Good News for you today—and that's "Good News" with a capital G and a capital N. Want to know what that Good News is? It's this: Jesus saves.

*Some of you just shrugged inwardly when I said that, and here's why: You've heard that Good News so many times, it seems commonplace to you. It's no longer capitalized, but lowercased—good news with a small "g" and a small "n." But I'm here to tell you that **we can remember with joy the*** *good news that Jesus saves! And to help us do that, let's try a little exercise right now.*

Instruct your listeners to take out their index cards and pencils and to turn to 1 Thessalonians 5:9-11 in the Bible.

Say: *Take the next few minutes to write yourself a letter that is a paraphrase of this passage of Scripture. At the top of your index card, write "Dear Me," and then rewrite the Bible verses in your own words, just for you. And don't worry; no one else will see what you write, so relax and enjoy yourself while you do this exercise.*

Give folks a little time to work on their paraphrases. Then say:

> **Tip**
>
> If you are unable to provide Bibles for those who don't have them, then you'll want to be sure to print out 1 Thessalonians 5:9-11 on a PowerPoint slide or transparency and to display that passage in a place where everyone can see it.

OK, wrap up your work and place your index card in an envelope. Go ahead and seal the envelope as well. Then write your own address on the front of the envelope.

When they've finished, tell people that during the coming week you want to help them encourage themselves with the news that Jesus saves. Ask ushers to gather the envelopes, and promise your group members that you'll mail them their own "letters from God"—that is, their own paraphrases of the good news of 1 Thessalonians 5:9-11. Close this exercise by saying:

When you receive your letter from God this week, let it be a joyful reminder for you of the Good News that Jesus saves!

P.S. Don't forget to mail out the envelopes first thing on Monday morning!

21

Bursting Point

Risk Rating: Medium

Scripture: 2 Thessalonians 3:16

Key Verse: "May the Lord of peace himself give you his peace at all times" (2 Thessalonians 3:16a).

Theme: Stress

Point: The best stress reliever is an ever-deepening relationship with the Lord of peace himself.

Synopsis: Audience members will blow up balloons to indicate the pressure they feel in stressful situations.

Supplies: One balloon for each person in your congregation

Preparation: Acquire your supplies ahead of time, and pray for God to bless your teaching efforts today.

Have ushers distribute one uninflated balloon to each person in the congregation. (The offering plates are a good way to distribute them; just fill them up with balloons and pass the plates up and down the pews with instructions for everyone to take a balloon out of the plate as it passes.) Say:

In a moment, I'm going to read a list of stressful situations. Each time you hear a situation similar to one you experienced in the past week, blow a deep breath into your balloon.

Warn your congregation that some balloons may pop during this activity—and that's OK. Then begin reading this list:

1. Got in an argument with a family member.

2. Workload felt overwhelming.

3. Got stuck in traffic.

4. Was late for an appointment.

5. Got an unexpected bill.

6. Felt ill.

7. Didn't get enough sleep.

8. Broke something at home.

9. Car broke down or had a flat tire.

10. Was reprimanded.

11. Had to prepare for a test.

12. Failed at something.

13. My checkbook didn't balance.

14. Had to travel away from my family for an extended time.

15. My favorite team lost a sporting event.

16. Realized I had fallen short of a biblical goal for my life.

17. Broke a commandment.

18. Got a traffic or parking ticket.

19. Lost my temper.

20. Felt afraid.

21. Felt discouraged.

22. Felt hurt by the someone's actions.

23. Felt like giving up on something or someone.

24. Worried about something.

25. Worried that I was worrying too much.

> **Tip**
>
> It's possible that a few people in your congregation may have allergies to balloons, so before starting this activity be sure to warn anyone in that situation not to participate in this exercise.

When you have finished reading the list, have participants hold up their balloons (or what's left of their balloons) so all can see the variety of stress levels represented within the congregation. Say:

As you can see, we all feel stress from a lot of different sources! But there is always one place we can go to find relief when we feel stressed: directly into the arms of God. Listen to what the Scripture says.

Read aloud 2 Thessalonians 3:16. Pause for emphasis, and then tell your listeners you want them to really hear what the Bible is trying to say to them today, and read it again. Wrap up the experience by saying:

The best stress reliever is an ever-deepening relationship with the Lord of peace himself. *Only then can we experience peace, no matter what.*

Then, just for fun and as an illustration of God's stress-relieving power, tell congregation members to let go of their balloons and send them flying all over the auditorium. (Be sure to get a few volunteers to help clean up after the service!)

IDEA 22

Les Misérables

Risk Rating: Low

Scripture: 1 Timothy 1:13-16

Key Verse: "Christ Jesus came into the world to save sinners" (1 Timothy 1:15b).

Theme: Mercy

Point: No one is beyond the reach of God's mercy.

Synopsis: Audience members will view a clip from the film *Les Misérables*.

Supplies: A DVD version of the 1998 film *Les Misérables* (rated PG-13, starring Liam Neeson) and the ability to show a clip from this DVD to the congregation

Preparation: Acquire your supplies ahead of time, and pray for God to bless your teaching efforts today. The film clip for this experience is located in track 4 on the DVD, beginning about six and a half minutes from the start of the movie (right at the beginning of track 4). This clip runs from time counter point 0:06:22 through 0:09:54 (the end of track 4). Please be sure to preview this clip to make sure its content is appropriate for your congregation.

At the appropriate time during your sermon, introduce the clip from *Les Misérables* by saying:

The classic story Les Misérables *was written by Victor Hugo. In 1998 Liam Neeson starred in a film adaptation of that book, and I'd like for us to watch a short scene from that film now.*

Liam Neeson plays Jean Valjean, a man who had been imprisoned for

19 years for stealing a loaf of bread. When he finally escapes, he is taken in by a priest who gives him food and a place to sleep. In the middle of the night, however, Jean Valjean decides to repay the priest's kindness by stealing his silver. Let's watch what happens next…

Show the clip; then pause for a moment to allow the scene to sink in. Ask congregation members to reflect on these questions:

• *What's your initial reaction to what you just saw? Why?*

• *What emotions do you think the priest felt after he'd been beaten and robbed by Jean Valjean?*

• *What emotions do you think Jean Valjean felt after he'd been set free—and enriched—by the priest?*

• *In what ways is this scene from* Les Misérables *a reflection of God's mercy in our lives today?*

Say: **No one is beyond the reach of God's mercy.** *Jean Valjean learned that in the fictional setting of* Les Misérables, *but the Apostle Paul learned that in real life. Listen to the way he described his experience.*

Read 1 Timothy 1:13-16 aloud to your congregation. Then continue your sermon as planned.

> **Tip**
>
> In general, federal copyright laws do not allow you to use videos or DVDs (even ones you own) for any purpose other than home viewing. Though some exceptions allow for the use of short segments of copyrighted material for educational purposes, it's best to be on the safe side. Your church can obtain a license from Christian Video Licensing for a small fee. Just visit www.cvli.org or call 1-888-771-2854 for more information. When using a movie that is not covered by the license, we recommend directly contacting the movie studio to seek permission to use the clip.

> **Tip**
>
> If your congregants are comfortable doing so, have them each find a friend and discuss their responses to the debriefing questions in pairs or small groups.

Million-Dollar Blessings

Risk Rating: Medium

Scripture: 1 Timothy 6:6-11

Key Verse: "True godliness with contentment is itself great wealth" (1 Timothy 6:6).

Theme: Money

Point: True godliness with contentment is great wealth.

Synopsis: Audience members will imagine what it would be like to spend $60 million for their church.

Supplies: Index cards and pencils

Preparation: Acquire your supplies ahead of time, and pray for God to bless your teaching efforts today.

Have members of the congregation form pairs or trios. Have ushers distribute index cards and pencils to each group in the congregation. Say:

At this point I would like to ask you and your partners to brainstorm together. Imagine that someone in our congregation has passed away, and in his will he designated that $60 million from his estate be donated to our church. Now it is your job to decide what our church should do with that money. Take a moment or two right now to brainstorm with your partners, and jot down your best ideas on your index card.

After allowing time for brainstorming, have ushers collect the index cards and give a stack of them to you. Spend a few minutes reading aloud some of the more entertaining or imaginative ideas on the cards. Then say:

Believe it or not, this exact situation did happen at the United Methodist Church in St. Mary's, Georgia. A parishioner of this 715-member *congregation passed away and left $60 million to his church. The only trouble was, the church didn't really need that huge amount of money, and they believed the Apostle Paul's words in 1 Timothy 6:6-11.*

Read aloud the Bible passage to your congregation. Then say:

I imagine that some of you are wondering what this little church did with that big wad of cash. Well, they decided to give it away. They used about $3 million to set up an endowment fund in the name of the deceased. The other $57 million they donated to other charities outside the church.

Next ask pairs to discuss these questions:

• *Do you think the United Methodist Church of St. Mary's, Georgia, did the right thing with that $60 million blessing? Defend your answer.*

Tip

If the people in your care are genuinely opposed to talking with others during church, then feel free to ask your congregants to brainstorm ideas individually instead of talking about them with others.

• *What do you think is the best approach for money management in a Christian's life?*

• *First Timothy teaches us that **true godliness with contentment is great wealth.** But what do you think that really means for you and me today? Explain.*

After discussion, continue your sermon as planned.

Pop Quiz!

Risk Rating: Low

Scripture: Titus 3:4-7

Key Verse: "He saved us, not because of the righteous things we had done, but because of his mercy" (Titus 3:5a).

Theme: Heaven

Point: We can never earn our way into heaven by doing good things.

Synopsis: Audience members will take a pop quiz to reveal their inability to achieve heaven on their own effort.

Supplies: None

Preparation: Pray for God to bless your teaching efforts today.

At the appropriate time in your sermon (preferably near the beginning), cheerfully announce that today you've decided to give everyone a pop quiz. Have congregation members stand up, and tell them to score their own quizzes on the honor system. Tell them that each question is worth 10 points, and anyone who scores 100 points will get a standing ovation from the rest of the congregation. Then ask the following *six* questions:

1. If you did a favor for someone during the past week, give yourself 10 points.

2. If you smiled at someone here at church this morning, give yourself 10 points.

3. If, at least once during the last week, you resisted the urge to tell a fib and told the truth instead, give yourself 10 points.

4. If you have ever gone on a mission trip—either short term or long term—give yourself 10 points.

5. If you have ever volunteered time in a church ministry anywhere, give yourself 10 points.

Pause and ask for a show of hands from people who think they might be doing pretty well on this quiz. Then continue:

6. If you have ever memorized a Bible verse—any verse at all—give yourself 10 points.

At this point, cheerfully—and abruptly—end the pop quiz by saying:

OK! That's it! If you scored 100 points, then remain standing for your ovation! If you scored 99 points or fewer, sit down because you didn't quite measure up to the standard.

Since it was possible to score only 60 points, everyone should sit down. Act surprised when you see that no one earned the standing ovation, and then say:

> **Tip**
>
> Because there may be non-Christians in attendance at your church service, be sure not to single anyone out after announcing the last question. Also make sure to include everyone in the standing ovation regardless of how he or she may have answered the last question on the quiz.

Well, it appears as though all your good deeds were not enough to earn you the coveted award of a standing ovation from your peers. Interestingly enough, we are all in a similar situation when it comes to heaven. The standard for getting into heaven is perfect sinlessness—and, even with all our good deeds—we can never measure up to that standard. But, you see, the Bible teaches us that God knew this and intervened on our behalf.

Read aloud Titus 3:4-7, with an emphasis on verse 5. Then say:

We can never earn our way into heaven by doing good things, *but God showed us his kindness and love and made heaven available to us simply because he loves us. So, in honor of God's provision, let's add one more question to our pop quiz—and this one will be worth 100 points all by itself.*

Have everyone stand. Say:

If you believe and accept the truth of Titus 3:4-7, then give yourself 100 points and rejoice because God has prepared heaven for you. And then, before anyone sits down, let's give ourselves a big round of applause to celebrate God's loving provision for each and every one of us!

25

Posture of Prayer

Risk Rating: Medium

Scripture: Philemon 4-21

Key Verse: "I appeal to you to show kindness" (Philemon 10a).

Theme: Praying for Others

Point: As Christians, we have the great privilege of pleading that kindness be bestowed on others.

Synopsis: Audience members will let their postures reflect the focus of their prayers.

Supplies: None

Preparation: Pray for God to bless your teaching efforts today.

At the appropriate time in your sermon, say: *As Christians, we have the great privilege of pleading that kindness be bestowed on others. The Apostle Paul was himself an example of this in his relationship with Onesimus, a runaway slave, and Philemon, the slave's owner.*

Spend a few minutes explaining Paul's efforts on behalf of Onesimus. This man had run away from his master—and ended up becoming a Christian and serving Paul in prison. Eventually, Paul sent him back to his master, Philemon, with a letter pleading for the master to be kind in spite of the slave's disobedience. That letter is now the book of Philemon in the Bible.

Next, use this physical prayer picture to bring home the news that just as Paul interceded on behalf of a runaway slave, we can offer prayer on behalf of others in need.

Then explain that you are going to lead the congregation in what is known as a posture prayer as a way to imitate Paul's example. Encourage your people to follow your directions to the extent they feel comfortable doing so, but not to let a little discomfort keep them from participating fully in the posture prayer experience. Then have everyone stand for prayer. Say:

To begin, please bow your head and spend a few moments praying silently for those in the world who are oppressed. Include those unable to worship freely, those terrorized by more powerful groups, and those who cannot hold their heads high and walk in freedom. Mention these people by name, if you can.

Allow a moment for people to pray; then continue:

Now sit down and pray for those who are unable to stand; those who have disabilities; and those who are challenged physically, mentally, emotionally, and in other ways. Mention these people by name, if you can.

> **Tip**
>
> This activity has proven to be a very moving experience for participants. If some in your congregation have a strongly emotional response to this prayer time, be flexible and allow time for people to process their feelings before you move on with your sermon.

After a few minutes say:

Now kneel and pray for the small people of the world—children. Pray for their hearts to be turned to Jesus. Pray that their parents or other adult care-givers would love them and cherish them in ways that bring honor to God and health to their souls. Pray that they will grow up physically healthy, that they will receive adequate education to succeed in their future careers, and that they will find great joy and satisfaction in their family relationships as they grow to adulthood. Again, mention these children by name if you can.

Again, allow time for silent prayer; then continue:

Put your face as close to the ground as possible and pray for those who are weak and those who cannot pray for themselves. Pray for those who are sick and those who are unborn.

After a few minutes, say:

Remain in this position and thank God for every opportunity you've had to show love to a person who was weak or without a voice.

Pause; then continue:

Now return to a kneeling position and offer thanks for the children God has put in your life—your own kids, younger relatives, children of your friends, and the children in your neighborhood. Thank God for giving you the opportunity to show his love to these little ones.

Pause; then continue:

Return to your seat, and as you sit, thank God for you life. No matter how frail and imperfect our bodies are, we have been given eternal life in Jesus. Thank God for that.

After a moment of thanks, continue:

Now stand with your head bowed and thank God for the freedom you have. Even if you feel oppressed in some part of your life, you have the freedom to pray right now and freedom from sin in Jesus. Thank God for his mercy and forgiveness.

Close this prayer time by asking God to help the people of your church remember to plead for kindness to be bestowed upon those in need. Then continue your sermon as planned.

make your message
stick...in pastoral staff and board meetings

In this section you'll find 15 creative activities to use during pastoral staff and board meetings. The ideas vary in style and content, but all conform to the following standards:

• They are drawn from specific Scripture passages and themes.

• They somehow involve everyone in the learning experience.

• They are appropriate for groups of just about any size, from three to 300 people.

• They can be done with few (or no) props and simple preparation.

Like the pulpit illustrations, debriefing and partner discussions are often a part of these illustrations. Unlike congregations, staff and board members are used to interacting in small groups, so we have assumed it will not be a problem for your staff members to debrief the activities together.

In the pulpit section, partner discussions automatically warranted a medium-risk rating. Not so in this section, so be prepared for that. And remember, you know your people best, so feel free to tailor these ideas to fit their personalities and comfort levels.

Thanks for your willingness to mentor and train people who will change the world.

IDEA 26

Love List

Risk Rating: Low

Scripture: Romans 12:9-10

Key Verse: "Love each other with genuine affection" (Romans 12:10a).

Theme: Relationships

Point: With God's help, we can live out Romans 12:9-10 in our relationships with co-workers in ministry.

Synopsis: Staff members will create a visual aid to help them evaluate their practice of biblical love.

Supplies: Paper and pencils

Preparation: Acquire your supplies ahead of time, and pray for God to bless your teaching efforts today.

Give each person a sheet of paper and a pencil, and tell people to make a list of up to 10 co-workers who participate in their ministry efforts at your church. Encourage them to include pastoral staff, volunteer leaders, board members, elders, deacons, technical staff (such as sound engineers, musicians, or video producers), and others on their lists. Remind folks that their list is not necessarily a "top 10" list and not to worry about ranking people on their lists, but rather to simply write down the first 10 names that come to mind when thinking about partners in ministry at your church. Also, be sure that participants understand that their lists are confidential and not meant to be shared with others in the group.

When your team is finished, say:

Now take a moment to review your list of names. Imagine that your paper represents your relationships with the ministry partners you've listed.

Read aloud Romans 12:9-10, and say:

This passage of Scripture reveals the governing principle behind all relationships—especially relationships with our co-workers in ministry. With that in mind, take your pencil and poke a hole in your paper for every time you've done any of the following:

• *spoken unkindly about one of these people behind his or her back.*

• *spoken sharply to one of these people.*

• *felt jealous or envious of one of these people's accomplishments in ministry.*

• *acted unkindly or deceptively toward one of these people.*

• *emphasized your own superiority and position at our church over one of these people in overt or subtle ways.*

• *joined with one of these people in gossiping or insulting another person who works with you in ministry.*

• *insisted on your own way without considering how it would affect one of the people on your list.*

Have team members count the number of holes in their papers, and then fold their papers so that no one else can see the names on them. Next, have your staff members find a partner to discuss these questions:

• *What's your initial reaction to seeing the holes poked in the names on your sheet?*

• *How are the holes in these papers a symbol of our relationships with our ministry partners?*

• *What does this exercise tell us about our efforts to love our co-workers in simple, practical ways?*

Have partners read Romans 12:9-10 to each other. Then ask them to discuss their responses to these questions:

• *What makes it difficult for us to allow this verse to govern our relationships with our co-workers in ministry? What might be done about that this week?*

Wrap up this exercise by saying:

*None of us is perfect, but **with God's help we can live out Romans 12:9-10 in our relationships with co-workers in ministry.** Let's agree to do just that this week.*

Then continue with your staff meeting as planned.

Doors of Foolishness

Risk Rating: Medium

Scripture: 1 Corinthians 1:18-31

Key Verse: "God has made the wisdom of this world look foolish" (1 Corinthians 1:20b).

Theme: Wisdom

Point: We will sometimes be considered fools for preaching the gospel of Christ.

Synopsis: Staff members will create a surprising shape with only paper and scissors.

Supplies: A sheet of paper and a pair of scissors for each participant.

Preparation: Acquire your supplies ahead of time, and pray for God to bless your teaching efforts today. You will also want to practice this activity ahead of time so that you can be confident of success and can help others with the activity.

At the appropriate time during your staff meeting, read 1 Corinthians 1:18-31 aloud to your team. Say:

*Scripture makes it clear that **we will sometimes be considered fools for preaching the gospel of Christ.** But we must always remember that when God is involved, things are not always as they seem.*

Distribute a sheet of paper and a pair of scissors to each person on your team.

Show everyone the plain sheet of paper and say:

If I were to say today that the only people who could work on our church staff were ones who could walk through this small piece of paper, you would all consider it foolishness no matter how much you might respect me. Like the gospel, that idea violates both our sensibilities and logic. But I'm here to tell you that your jobs are safe—it can be done! In fact, we are going to create doors of paper together, right now.

Proceed by leading each of your team members in the steps shown in the illustration on page 90. Take your time as you lead folks through this, verifying each step with staff members as you proceed. You may also want to have a few spare sheets of paper in case someone makes an irreversible mistake on his or her first try. When you are finished with the cutting steps, you will be able to open the paper into a large, door-shaped rectangle— one that is large enough for an adult person to walk through.

> **Tip**
>
> If scissors are in short supply, or if you think your staff members will simply work better in teams, feel free to have participants work in pairs as you lead this activity.

Have everyone display his or her paper doors and then take turns walking through the paper to prove it can be done. Then say:

What seemed like foolishness—walk through a piece of paper—at the beginning of this activity is now clearly a very real option. As we have all seen, it is in fact possible to walk through a single sheet of paper. But it takes a different kind of wisdom than conventional wisdom—it takes a wisdom that appears to be foolish in order to accomplish this task. Likewise, Jesus Christ is our only door to eternal life. That appeared to be foolishness to the Corinthians, and it continues to seem illogical and unwise to many people today. But this gospel of Christ was true then, and it's true today—no matter what the so-called wise people may say. Let's take courage in that good news as we share the good news with others this week.

Continue your staff meeting as planned.

Walk Through a Piece of Paper

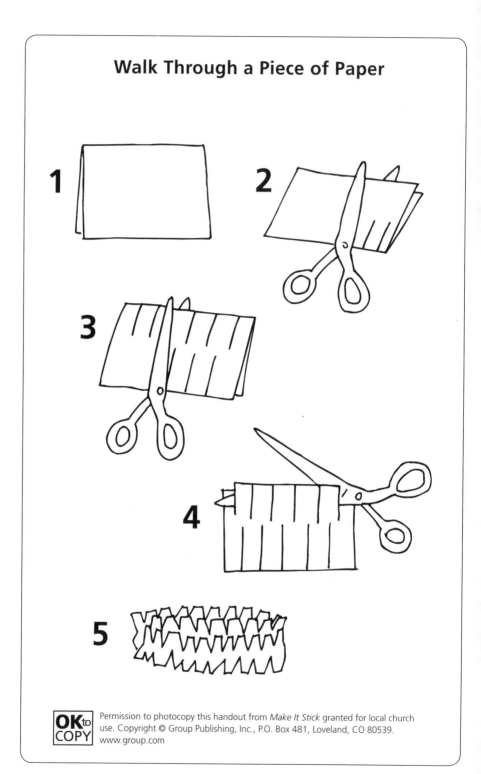

Q & A With a Bible

Risk Rating: Medium

Scripture: 1 Corinthians 2

Key Verse: "We have received God's Spirit…so we can know the wonderful things God has freely given us" (1 Corinthians 2:12).

Theme: Questions

Point: Pursuing questions about Scripture opens a window of opportunity for God's Holy Spirit to teach us truth.

Synopsis: Staff members will practice asking—and answering—questions about Scripture.

Supplies: An index card and pencil for each participant

Preparation: Acquire your supplies ahead of time, and pray for God to bless your teaching efforts today.

Gather your staff around a table, and give everyone an index card and pencil. Say:

At this point in our meeting, I'd like us to do a little Q & A exercise with Scripture.

Instruct each staff member to open a Bible to 1 Corinthians 2. Tell participants to take the next few minutes to read this chapter of Scripture and to jot down on their index cards any questions that come to mind as they read. Suggest that these should be questions they might ask Jesus himself if he were sitting at the table with you. Encourage everyone to come up with at least five questions triggered by the reading.

When everyone is ready, have each person place a star next to one or two questions they felt were most intriguing or that most piqued their curiosity. Collect the index cards and mix them up in your hands.

Next, say a brief prayer asking God's Holy Spirit to reveal truth to your team during the rest of this exercise.

Tip

Some staff members who are more auditory in their learning style may have trouble splitting their concentration between reading and writing. If this seems to be the case with several of your staffers, offer to read aloud 1 Corinthians 2 while the others listen and jot down their questions. If you opt to do this, you'll probably want to read the chapter aloud at least twice.

After prayer, select a thought-provoking question from the top index card, and read it aloud to the group. Say:

Obviously, Jesus isn't sitting at this table with us in physical form. However, his Holy Spirit is always present with us. So, with that in mind, let's continue this exercise by tackling this question ourselves to see what kind of truth we can discover as we try to answer it from Christ's perspective.

Encourage discussion about the question, but don't let the conversation become belabored. Help your team to explore possible responses—and also communicate that it's OK if no definitive answer is reached. After a few minutes, move the discussion toward a starred question on the second card. Continue discussing as many starred questions as time and interest allow.

Afterward, ask:

• *How did it make you feel to be challenged to ask questions about the Bible? Explain.*

• *What benefits did we gain as a pastoral team from this Q & A session with Scripture?*

• *What important insights might we have missed if we had neglected to raise questions about the Scripture we read?*

• *What can we learn from this experience that can help us in our future studies of Scripture? in the way we teach our congregation truth from Scripture?*

Finish this exercise by saying:

Pursuing questions about Scripture opens a window of opportunity for God's Holy Spirit to teach us truth. *In the days to come, let's challenge each other to become expert question askers—and people who depend on the Holy Spirit to reveal God's truth as a result.*

Pie Charts

Risk Rating: Medium

Scripture: 1 Corinthians 9:19-23

Key Verse: "I have become a slave to all people to bring many to Christ" (1 Corinthians 9:19b).

Theme: The Church

Point: A healthy church exhibits a healthy balance between the elements of worship, instruction, community, and outreach.

Synopsis: Staff members will explore the priorities of ministry by creating and discussing paper-plate pie charts.

Supplies: A paper plate and pen for each participant

Preparation: Acquire your supplies ahead of time, and pray for God to bless your teaching efforts today.

Give everyone a paper plate and a pen. Say:

A healthy church exhibits a healthy balance between the elements of worship, instruction, community, and outreach. Today, I'd like us to explore what that might mean for us at our church.

On the front of their paper plates, have everyone draw a pie chart that represents the ideal percentages of a church staff's time, budget, and energies that each element of a healthy church warrants. For example, if someone thinks that worship takes more effort to achieve a roughly similar result as other ministries, he or she might relegate 50 percent of the pie chart to worship and split the remaining 50 percent among the other three emphases. Give everyone a minute or two to complete the exercise, then have staff members take turns explaining how they determined their percentages. Allow group members to pass if others have already shared similar percentages.

Next, have staff members turn their paper plates over and make new pie charts that represent the way they view your church's *actual* allocation of resources in the areas of worship, instruction, community, and outreach. Afterward, have staff members compare their original pie charts with the new pie charts and discuss why they are similar or different. Use these questions to help prompt discussions:

• *What accounts for the similarities and differences in our pie charts?*

• *In what ways do our own personal priorities affect the way we view our church's priorities? And is that good or bad? Explain.*

• *In our church we have people who need a stronger emphasis on one element of a healthy church than another, and often their needs change according to their life situations. How does that—or should that—affect the healthy balance of ministry that our church staff attempts to provide?*

Say: *In 1 Corinthians 9:19-23 the Apostle Paul gave an example of a church leader's responsibilities to minister to people of varying needs.*

Read aloud the Bible passage; then ask:

• *How realistic do you think Paul's example is in relation to our ministry efforts here? Defend your answer.*

• *Based on this passage, what kind of pie chart do you think Paul might draw?*

• *What's one thing we can do this week to help live out 1 Corinthians 9:19-23 in the way we attempt to conduct a balanced, healthy ministry to the people in our church?*

Continue with your staff meeting as planned.

Life on the Scales

Risk Rating: Medium

Scripture: 1 Corinthians 10:23-24, 31

Key Verse: "Do it all for the glory of God"
(1 Corinthians 10:31b).

Theme: Balance

Point: We glorify God by living balanced, faithful lives.

Synopsis: Staff members will create an object to prompt discussion on leading a balanced lifestyle.

Supplies: None

Preparation: Pray for God to bless your teaching efforts today.

At the appropriate time in your staff meeting, begin a discussion about balance, faithfulness, and burnout in ministry leaders. Ask your staff members to make a quick personal inventory of all their major responsibilities in the upcoming week, including family responsibilities, ministry responsibilities, friendship responsibilities, and spiritual responsibilities. Then read aloud 1 Corinthians 10:23-24, 31. Say:

We glorify God by living balanced, faithful lives within the context of our responsibilities. All too often, however, our lives become unbalanced when our obligations and commitments pile up on us.

Tell everyone that you'd like to try a little experiment to help your team get a visual impression of what you're talking about. Have participants stand up and hold their arms straight out from their sides. (People will probably need to move apart to avoid bumping into each other.) Then say:

Imagine that your body is an old-fashioned scale or balance, the kind with a tray for weights on each side. I'm going to read several statements. If any statement applies to you, follow the directions to move your arms up or down as indicated.

Read the following directions:

• If you worked at your job this week, move your right arm up six inches and your left arm down six inches.

• For each family member of yours who needed personal attention this week, move your right arm up six inches and your left arm down six inches.

• If you took time out for personal refreshment or recreation this week, move your left arm up six inches and your right arm down six inches.

• For every evening you spent at an obligation away from home this week, move your right arm up six inches and your left arm down six inches.

• If you shortchanged your spiritual time this week, stand on your right leg and raise your right arm six inches and lower your left arm six inches.

• For each friend who needed special attention this week, move your right arm up six inches and your left arm down six inches.

• For each night you slept well and woke up refreshed, move your left arm up six inches and your right arm down six inches.

• For each night you slept poorly or felt like you didn't sleep long enough, move your right arm up six inches and your left arm down six inches.

• If sometime during this week you faced an unexpected demand that felt like the straw that broke the camel's back, move your right arm up six inches and your left arm down six inches.

Have your team members hold their positions for about 15 seconds; then allow them to return to their seats. Have staffers find a partner to discuss these questions:

• How was this activity like or unlike trying to maintain balance in life?

• Based on your final position, how would you rate yourself at living out a balanced lifestyle last week? Use a scale of 1 to 10 (with 10 being the most balanced rating), and explain why you rated yourself that way.

• How would you describe a perfectly balanced life that "does it all for the glory of God"?

• What obstacles prevent you from experiencing weeks like that? What can you do about it?

Have pairs take a few moments to share with the group at large any insights they discovered during their discussions. Then continue your staff meeting as planned.

It's Photocopied All Over Your Face

Risk Rating: High

Scripture: 1 Corinthians 13:12

Key Verse: "Now we see things imperfectly" (1 Corinthians 13:12a).

Theme: Truth

Point: We are imperfect teachers of a perfect truth.

Synopsis: Staff members will photocopy their faces and discuss truth.

Supplies: A photocopier machine and a hand mirror

Preparation: Acquire your supplies ahead of time, and pray for God to bless your teaching efforts today.

Begin this experience by reading aloud 1 Corinthians 13:12. Say:

As Christian leaders in our church, **we are imperfect teachers of a perfect truth,** *the Bible. But obviously we can't simply give up on teaching the truth because we are imperfect. So I'd like us to spend some time discussing this situation today.*

Ask your team to respond to these questions:

• *What does this Scripture say to you about God's truth? Explain.*

• *What makes it difficult for us to grasp real truth?*

• *With this Scripture in mind, what do you think is our responsibility when teaching truth to the people in our spiritual care?*

After discussion, say:

I'm going to take you out of your comfort zone now—so get ready to do something you wouldn't normally do!

Lead your team to a photocopier machine; then tell them you want them all to take turns making photocopies of their faces. Warn everyone to be sure to keep their eyes tightly closed during the photocopying process to avoid retinal damage that could be caused by looking at the light with unprotected eyes. Then lead by example: Plaster your face on the copy machine and make a photocopy of your face. Have other staff members take turns (safely) doing the same. Then have everyone take his or her photocopy back to your meeting area.

When everyone is back in place, have them each look closely at their photocopies while you reread 1 Corinthians 13:12. Ask:

• *How is your picture in that photocopy like the way we view God's truth in this life?*

• *What percentage of your photocopy would you say is the true you? What percentage would you say is a distorted image of you?*

Pass around a hand mirror. Have team members compare the clear, true image of themselves in the hand mirror with the distorted ones. Then wrap up your time by asking team members to brainstorm answers to this question:

• *What can we, as pastoral staff members, do today to help present an undistorted image (or at least a more nearly perfect image) of God's truth to our people? What can we do tomorrow? next week? next year?*

32

Churches R Us

Risk Rating: Medium

Scripture: Ephesians 4:11-13

Key Verse: "Build up the church, the body of Christ" (Ephesians 4:12b).

Theme: Leadership

Point: As leaders of our local church, our responsibility is to build the Church by diligently building up the people within our own congregation.

Synopsis: Staff members will build models of a church and discuss church leadership.

Supplies: A variety of small, unexpected building supplies such as a few bricks, cardboard, scissors, masking tape, paper, and markers. Make sure you have enough of everything for every two people in your team meeting to have the same (or similar) items.

Preparation: Acquire your supplies ahead of time, and pray for God to bless your teaching efforts today.

At the appropriate time during your staff or board meeting, form pairs and distribute to each pair the building materials you've gathered. Make sure each group has similar (or the same) building supplies.

Say: *We're going to have a little fun now with this exercise, so get ready to use your creativity. You've all just become members of the church-building organization Churches R Us. With your partner, work to build a church right now. Be creative and have fun with this. Ready? Go.*

Have staff members use their supplies to build a model of a church. Encourage creativity and cooperation as staff members contribute to their buildings. Afterward, have a volunteer from each pair take turns presenting its church to the rest of the group.

After presentations, have pairs discuss the following questions:

• *What were you thinking during this exercise?*

• *What made it easy or difficult to build your church?*

• *How is the way you worked with your partner like the way the people of God work together as the church?*

• *In one sentence, how would you describe the way the Holy Spirit works to empower Christians to build the church?*

Tip

If it's inconvenient to bring unexpected building supplies (such as brick and cardboard), then simply raid your office supply cabinet and bring in items like index cards, staplers, transparent tape, and paper clips. The models these supplies yield won't be as impressive, but they will still serve the purpose well and will facilitate the learning experience just the same.

Have staff members share any insights gained from their discussions. Then say:

*It was challenging and fun to create a church out of these building materials, but God has created the Church (with a capital C) out of something more. God's Church is made up of the stuff of this group here—people like you, me, and all the other Christians in the world. **And as leaders of our local church, our responsibility is to build the Church by diligently building up the people within our own congregation.***

Have partners read Ephesians 4:11-13 together and then respond to these questions:

• *In what ways do we sometimes confuse the Church with buildings or programs?*

• *What are the dangers of de-emphasizing the human aspect of God's church?*

• *What does it mean to "build up the church, the body of Christ"?*

• *In tangible, practical terms, what is a Christian leader's responsibility in light of Ephesians 4:11-13?*

• *What can you and I do this week to be leaders who fulfill the goal of Ephesians 4:11-13?*

Have staff members share any insights they gained from their discussions, and then continue the meeting as planned.

IDEA 33

Sweet Service

Risk Rating: Low

Scripture: Philippians 2:3-4

Key Verse: "Don't look out only for your own interests" (Philippians 2:4a).

Theme: Motivation

Point: The privilege of serving God is its own reward.

Synopsis: Staff members will use candy bars to examine some of the reasons for serving God.

Supplies: A Dove chocolate for each participant and a brown paper bag containing one of each of the following candy bars: PayDay, 100 Grand, Mr. Goodbar, Snickers

Preparation: Acquire your supplies ahead of time, and pray for God to bless your teaching efforts today.

Place all the candy bars—except the Dove chocolates—in a brown paper bag. At the appropriate time in your meeting, begin a discussion that centers on the motivation for serving God through a role in church leadership. Then show the bag to your team, and tell your staff members that each item in the bag represents a reason people have for serving God. Ask for volunteers to each select one item from the bag, pausing to talk about each item before a new one is drawn. As the candy bars are drawn out, make the following observations:

   • *PayDay—Some people are motivated to serve God by the desire to gain the reward of an eternal payday: a home in heaven.*

   • *100 Grand—Some people are motivated to serve God by the desire for prosperity in this life. Prosperity may include both financial blessings and emotional significance.*

• *Mr. Goodbar—Some people are motivated to serve God primarily by the desire to simply be good, moral people.*

• *Snickers—Some people are motivated to serve God primarily by the exhilaration and joy found in a relationship with God.*

Encourage your team members to brainstorm other ways the candy bars might represent motivations to serve God. Then say:

All of these candy bars represent something we get out of serving God in our church and in our lives. None of the things mentioned are inherently wrong motivations. God does promise eternal life. He also promises abundant life that sometimes shows itself in financial or emotional prosperity. And he empowers us to live morally upright lives and lives filled with his joy.

*However, as we serve God in our respective roles within this church, we need to remember that none of these fringe benefits should be the heart of our motivation for service. **The privilege of serving God is its own reward**, and we do that best by relying on the Holy Spirit to help us help others in our congregation.*

Distribute Dove chocolates to participants as a reminder to depend on the Holy Spirit to motivate their ministry efforts. Then read aloud Philippians 2:3-4, with emphasis on verse 4. Wrap up your meeting by encouraging participants to live out this passage's advice as they approach their ministries this week.

IDEA 34

What I Think About Me

Risk Rating: Medium

Scripture: Philippians 3:4-21

Key Verse: "We are citizens of heaven"
(Philippians 3:20a).

Theme: Self-Image

Point: We are citizens of heaven.

Synopsis: Staff members will explore Paul's self-image and create their own personality profiles.

Supplies: A photocopy of the "What I Think About Me" handout (pp. 105-106) and a pencil for each participant

Preparation: Acquire your supplies ahead of time, and pray for God to bless your teaching efforts today.

At the appropriate time during your staff meeting, ask team members to offer their responses to this question:

• *What influence over a ministry do you think a pastoral staff member's self-image might have?*

Encourage your staff members to brainstorm both positive and negative influences in response to that question. Then say:

Let's take a moment to think about some of the Apostle Paul's experiences and explore how they might have influenced his self-image and ministry.

Have your team turn to Philippians 3, and ask a volunteer to read aloud verses 4 through 6. Then ask:

• *How would you describe Paul's self-image before he came to Christ?*

• *To what extent was Paul's self-image accurate?*

Have another volunteer read aloud Philippians 3:7-21. Then ask your team members to find a partner and discuss these questions:

• How did Paul's self-image change after meeting Christ? In what ways did it stay the same?

• How do you think Paul's self-image, as described in Philippians 3, influenced his subsequent ministry efforts and effectiveness? Explain.

• What can we, as leaders in our church, learn from Paul's experience?

• What happens when Christian leaders buy into a flawed set of beliefs about themselves? when they see themselves as God sees them?

Have pairs share with the whole team any insights they gained from their discussions. Then give everyone a pencil and a copy of the handout "What I Think About Me" (pp. 105-106). Tell staff members you'd like them to use the handout to write personality profiles of themselves, which they will then share with a partner. Allow time for your team members to complete the handout and to share their profiles with a partner. Then say:

*The Apostle Paul has given us both a great example and great wisdom to follow. **We are citizens of heaven,** and we need to let that truth define our self-images so that we can approach our personal ministries with a healthy, humble, and confident determination to serve Jesus Christ.* •

What I Think About Me

Create a personality profile of yourself by supplying the information requested for each category. Answer as honestly as you can. You'll be sharing your answers with your partner in several minutes.

My name:

My parents' names:

Three adjectives I'd use to describe myself:

One thing my mother taught me:

One thing my father taught me:

My two greatest weaknesses as a person:

My two greatest strengths as a person:

My two most important goals in life:

The toughest part of my faith journey:

The best thing about being a Christian:

One thing from my past I wish I could forget:

Matchsticks

Risk Rating: High

Scripture: Philippians 4:6-7

Key Verse: "His peace will guard your hearts and minds" (Philippians 4:7b).

Theme: Burnout

Point: We don't have to let stress and feelings of burnout dominate us or our work for the Lord Jesus.

Synopsis: Staff members will use matches to explore feelings of stress and burnout.

Supplies: A matchbook for every six participants, a candle, a sheet of paper, and a pencil

Preparation: Acquire your supplies ahead of time, and pray for God to bless your teaching efforts today.

Show the matchbooks to everyone on your team. Then select one person in your group to act as a scribe who records the staff members' contributions during the activity.

Next, give these instructions:

While maintaining the utmost care and concern for safety, each person on our team will take turns lighting a match and then—before the match burns out—naming as many things as possible that cause stress and burnout in his or her life.

Hand a matchbook to the first person and begin. Have the scribe write down the items that are mentioned. When the first person's match burns out, pass the matchbook to another person on your staff and repeat the process. However, tell this second person that he or she can't duplicate any item that the first person already mentioned.

Continue until everyone has had a turn at holding a burning match. Be sure to let someone substitute for your scribe so he or she can also hold a match and contribute to the list your group is making.

After the matchbook has made it around to everyone in the meeting at least once, have the scribe read the completed list aloud. Then ask staffers to find a partner and discuss these questions:

• *How did you feel as you listed causes of stress while holding a burning match?*

• *How are those feelings similar to your feelings when you are under pressure in real life?*

• *What do you do to cope with feelings of stress and burnout?*

• *When is pressure good for you? When is it dangerous? Explain.*

Have partners take turns sharing with the whole group any insights gained from their discussions. Then say:

*We can't escape stress or occasionally feeling burned out in our lives and in our ministries. But **we don't have to let stress and feelings of burnout dominate us or our work for the Lord Jesus.***

Turn out all the lights, and place the candle in the middle of the room. Have whoever was last to hold a matchstick light the candle for your group. Then, by candlelight, read aloud Philippians 4:6-7. Afterward lead your team in a time of prayer about specific stress-inducers from your list, and ask for God's peace to dominate your lives and ministry at your church. Then continue your staff meeting as planned.

Tip

Even though this exercise utilizes matches in a way that most responsible adults will have no problem with, please show caution—and encourage your team members to show caution—in the handling of any flame. Keep a bowl of water nearby to douse used matchsticks, keep paper away from any flames, and take any other reasonable precautions to secure a safe learning environment for your team.

Tip

If there are more than eight people on your staff, consider having your staff form groups of four to six people each, and then have all the groups conduct the activity simultaneously. This will save time and allow for more varied discussion within groups afterward.

36

Thank You

Risk Rating: Medium

Scripture: Philippians 4:8-9

Key Verse: "Think about things that are excellent and worthy of praise" (Philippians 4:8b).

Theme: Team Building

Point: As leaders in our church, we have unique opportunities to encourage one another.

Synopsis: Staff members will write Scripture-based thank you cards to show appreciation for one another.

Supplies: A thank you card and pencil or pen for each participant

Preparation: Acquire your supplies ahead of time, and pray for God to bless your teaching efforts today.

Use this team-building activity to help your staff practice encouraging one another in their work and ministry at your church.

Gather your staff around a table, and give everyone a blank thank you card and a pencil. Have each person write his or her name on the envelope of the thank you card. Then ask everyone to listen as you read aloud Philippians 4:8-9. Say:

As leaders at our church, we would do well to follow Paul's advice in this passage and fill our minds with those things that are true, honorable, right, pure, lovely, admirable, excellent, and worthy of praise. Also, **as leaders in our church, we have unique opportunities to encourage one another** *while we follow Paul's advice. So that's what we're going to do today.*

Have everyone pass his or her thank you card and addressed envelope to the right. Say:

Look at the name on your envelope and take a moment to think about that person and the way he or she demonstrates what is true in life. Then on that person's card, write a short, one-sentence note of thanks that highlights this quality in your co-worker's life.

Pause a moment to allow team members to write their first notes. When everyone is ready, have people pass their cards to the right again and repeat the process, this time writing a one-sentence note of thanks that highlights something honorable in the appropriate person's life. Continue passing cards and writing notes until each card has a note addressing each of the rest of the qualities listed in Philippians 4:8 (right, pure, lovely, admirable, excellent, and worthy of praise). It's OK if the same person writes more than one note on a card.

When everyone is finished, have staff members return the cards to the appropriate people and take a few minutes to allow your team to read what was written about them. Then wrap up this team-building affirmation with a prayer of thanks, naming each person on your staff and thanking God for his or her unique contributions to the ministry of your church.

37

Up in the Air

Risk Rating: Medium

Scripture: Colossians 1:18-19

Key Verse: "He is first in everything"
(Colossians 1:18b).

Theme: Priorities

Point: Jesus is first in every situation.

Synopsis: Staff members will try to keep several balloons aloft at once as a visual demonstration of keeping priorities in order.

Supplies: One marker and three uninflated round balloons (one blue balloon and two yellow balloons) for each person and a watch or timer

Preparation: Acquire your supplies ahead of time, and pray for God to bless your teaching efforts today.

At the appropriate time during your staff meeting, distribute one blue balloon, one yellow balloon, and a marker to each participant. Then read aloud Colossians 1:18-19. Say:

We're going to try an experiment this morning to help us bring home the message of this Scripture. So first please inflate your blue balloon and tie it off. Then write "Jesus" in large letters on the balloon.

Pause while people follow your instructions. Then have them inflate their yellow balloons. On each of the yellow balloons, ask your pastoral team members to write only one of the following words that represent life priorities:

• Family
• Ministry

- Health
- Financial stewardship
- Community
- Looming deadlines
- Other

Tell staff members that they can choose only two of the priorities you listed (one for each yellow balloon). If someone chooses "other," have him or her describe that priority on the appropriate yellow balloon. When everyone is finished, he or she should have one blue balloon that says "Jesus" on it, and two yellow balloons that each has one other life priority written on it. Say:

For the next 60 seconds, I'd like you to try and juggle your balloons without letting any of them touch the floor or the table or a chair. Do everything you can to keep all three balloons in the air at all times—without getting up out of your seat. Ready? Begin.

When everyone is finished, discuss how well people managed to keep their balloon priorities in the air. Then have staff members repeat the activity; only this time tell them to hold the blue balloon firmly in one hand and then to juggle the two yellow balloons with the other hand. After 60 seconds assess how they fared the second time around. Then ask team members to find a partner to discuss these questions:

- *What went through your mind as you tried to juggle your balloon priorities while staying seated in your chair?*
- *What was the biggest difference for you between the first time you juggled balloons and the second time?*
- *Were you ever worried about dropping the blue balloon the second time*

around? Why or why not?

• *What might we learn from this exercise that could shed light on the way we live out Colossians 1:18-19?*

Wrap up this experience by saying:

*Keeping priorities in order is a challenge for everyone, especially for those of us in Christian leadership. As we minister to our congregation in the coming weeks, let's doggedly determine to daily hold to the truth of Colossians 1:18-19 and remember that **Jesus is first in every situation.***

38

Critical Issues

Risk Rating: Medium

Scripture: 1 Timothy 4:16

Key Verse: "Stay true to what is right"
(1 Timothy 4:16b).

Theme: Doctrine

Point: We need to continually concentrate on what is most important about the Christian faith.

Synopsis: Staff members will examine what they believe about basic Christian doctrine.

Supplies: A photocopy of the "Critical Issues" handout (p. 116) and a pencil for each participant

Preparation: Acquire your supplies ahead of time, and pray for God to bless your teaching efforts today.

At the appropriate time during your staff or board meeting, read aloud 1 Timothy 4:16. Then give each person a copy of the "Critical Issues" handout (p. 116) and a pencil. Say:

Few people in our church have the time and resources to explore every aspect of the Christian faith, so it's important that we as leaders know—and teach—what's really vital to our belief system. Take the next several minutes to complete your handout, and then choose a partner nearby to discuss the questions at the bottom. Be honest about your beliefs and sensitive to others as they express their opinions.

When people have had enough time to complete the handout and discuss the questions, ask staff members to report which statements they marked as "essential." Encourage participants to discuss areas of disagreement so they can understand each other as fully as possible. See if it's possible to achieve consensus among your team members on at least one (or more) "essential" doctrine as listed on the handout.

Wrap up this exploration by saying:

*If we intend to follow the instruction of 1 Timothy 4:16 in the way we lead this church body, **we need to continually concentrate on what is most important about the Christian faith.** Doing that allows us to stay true to what is right and gives us confidence to share Jesus with others.*

Critical Issues

Read the statements below and mark whether you think a person needs to believe them to be a Christian. If, in your opinion, a person must believe a statement in order to be a Christian, mark the "essential" box. If a statement is important but not absolutely necessary, mark the "important" box. If a statement is true but not crucial to your faith, mark the "not important" box. Finally, if you don't believe that a statement is true, mark the "not true" box.

When you've marked all the statements, find a partner and discuss the questions at the bottom of the handout.

	Essential	Important	Not important	Not true
1. Jesus is God's Son.				
2. The Bible is the unerring Word of God.				
3. Jonah was swallowed by a large fish.				
4. God will bless those who love him.				
5. Jesus walked on water.				
6. Jesus died on the cross.				
7. The Bible has the answers to all of life's questions.				
8. Jesus rose from the dead.				
9. Jesus turned water into wine.				
10. We were created to live in relationship with God.				
11. Moses parted the Red Sea.				
12. All good people will go to heaven.				
13. The world will end just as described in Revelation.				

Discussion Questions

- Which beliefs do you and your partner agree are essential?
- On which beliefs do you disagree regarding what's essential?
- In your opinion, why are the essential statements vital to the Christian faith?
- In your opinion, why are the other statements not essential?

Wordless Stories

Risk Rating: Medium

Scripture: 2 Timothy 4:1-2

Key Verse: "Preach the word of God" (2 Timothy 4:2a).

Theme: Sharing Faith

Point: "Preach the gospel at all times; if necessary, use words" (St. Francis of Assisi).

Synopsis: Staff members will try to communicate without using words.

Supplies: Paper and colored pencils

Preparation: Acquire your supplies ahead of time, and pray for God to bless your teaching efforts today.

Open your pastoral staff session by distributing paper and a few colored pencils to each person. Then have group members divide the space on their papers into four equal-sized quadrants, much like a four-panel cartoon. When everyone has done that, say:

Some of us have had a pretty good day today, some have had a bad day, and others have experienced everything in between. So we're going to start off our staff meeting by telling each other all about the day we've had today. There's one catch, though. For this exercise, we're not allowed to use words! So use your paper and pencils to tell the story of your day using pictures only. And don't worry, artistic ability is not required. Feel free to use stick figures or whatever other kinds of objects you need to communicate the story of your day.

Give staff members a few minutes to brainstorm, and then draw, the stories of their days. When everyone seems to be about finished, give a 60-second warning to allow group members to put the finishing touches on their drawings. Then have people take turns showing their pictures to the rest of the group. Encourage others to guess what the story of the day is based only on the pictures at first; then allow the artist to explain his or her drawings to the rest of the group.

Afterward, have staff members find a partner to discuss these questions:

Tip

This exercise works best at an evening staff meeting. However, if your staff is meeting during the day, then simply adjust the directions to refer to "yesterday" rather than "today."

• *What adjectives would you use to describe having to tell about your day without using words?*

• *What makes it difficult for you to communicate without words? What makes it easier?*

• *Read together 2 Timothy 4:1-2. Why do you suppose the Apostle Paul thought it so important for Timothy to "preach the word of God"?*

• *When words aren't available, what kind creative approaches can we use to tell the story of Jesus to people around us?*

• *What can we learn from this activity to help us accomplish the goals expressed in 2 Timothy 4:1-2 this week?*

Tip

If your staff is 12 or more people, you may want to save time by having staffers share their drawings with each other in pairs or trios rather than with the group as a whole.

After discussions, invite group members to share any insights they gained from talking with their partners. Then have group members write the words of 2 Timothy 4:2 somewhere on their drawings. Say:

Saint Francis of Assisi is credited with saying, **"Preach the gospel at all times; if necessary, use words."** *This week, let's place our drawings someplace at home that will remind us to do just that each and every day.*

Continue with the rest of your meeting as planned.

Follow the Leader

Risk Rating: Medium

Scripture: Titus 1:6-9

Key Verse: "An elder must live a blameless life" (Titus 1:6a).

Theme: Leadership

Point: Choosing a leader for our church body is a task not to be taken lightly.

Synopsis: Staff members will try to guess who the leader is during an activity.

Supplies: None

Preparation: Pray for God to bless your teaching efforts today.

Use this exercise when it's time to nominate new candidates for your church leadership team.

Have everyone stand up, spread out, and face the same direction in the room. Choose one volunteer to leave the room. When he or she has exited, designate another person to be the leader. Say:

When our volunteer returns, he (or she) will try to guess whom we've designated as our leader. Our job will be to follow the actions of our leader while trying not to let our volunteer know who the leader is. Don't look directly at anyone—especially our leader—but try to catch what our leader is doing out of the corner of your eye.

Instruct the leader to change his or her actions about every 10 or 15 seconds. Suggest that the leader do things such as crossing his or her arms, scratching his or her head, yawning, snapping his or her fingers, clapping, patting someone on the back, jumping up and down, and turning around.

When your team is ready, bring the volunteer back into the room, update him or her on the goal, and then start the exercise. Keep it going until the volunteer has correctly identified the designated leader. Then repeat the exercise with a different volunteer and a different leader. After several rounds, gather everyone around a table and ask:

• *What did you discover about leadership through this little exercise?*

• *What did you discover about following a leader?*

• *What made for a good leader in our exercise?*

Introduce the topic of nominating new leaders for your church, and ask:

• *What can we learn about choosing a leader for our church from this exercise?*

• *What makes for a good leader in our church setting?*

Read aloud Titus 1:6-9. Say: ***Choosing a leader for our church body is a task not to be taken lightly.*** Ask:

• *If you were to summarize in one sentence the character of a good leader based on the Apostle Paul's advice in this passage, what would you say?*

• *Before we make any decisions about whom to add to our leadership team, what can we decide about the process of choosing a leader that will help us stay informed of Titus 1:6-9 and the lessons we learned through this leadership exercise?*

Continue your meeting as planned.

make your message stick...in adult small-group and Sunday school settings

In this section you'll find 15 creative ideas for activities to use during adult small-group and Sunday school meetings. As before, the ideas vary in style and content, but all conform to the following standards:

• They are drawn from specific Scripture passages and themes.

• They somehow involve everyone in the group in the learning experience.

• They are appropriate for groups of just about any size, from three to 300 people.

• They can be done with few (or no) props and simple preparation.

Like the previous activities in this book, debriefing and partner discussions are often a part of these exercises. As in staff and board meetings, partner discussions and interaction are not unusual in this setting, and so they are generally considered a low risk. Still, you know your people best, so feel free to tailor these ideas to fit their personalities and comfort levels.

Thanks for being willing to change the world, one person at a time!

41

Frozen Clay

Risk Rating: Medium

Scripture: Romans 8:29

Key Verse: "He chose them to become like his Son" (Romans 8:29b).

Theme: Christ-likeness

Point: We have been chosen to become like Christ.

Synopsis: Learners will attempt to mold sculptures from frozen clay and compare that to the goal of becoming like Christ.

Supplies: One handful of modeling clay for each participant and the ability to freeze the clay and a watch or clock with a second hand

Preparation: Acquire your supplies ahead of time, and pray for God to bless your teaching efforts today.

The night before your small group or Sunday school class meets, gather enough modeling clay for each person in your group to have a handful. Separate the clay into individual portions; then place it in a freezer overnight.

At your small-group or Sunday school meeting, pass out one lump of frozen clay to every person, but tell people not to do anything with the clay until you give the instructions. When you're ready, say:

Take your lump of clay and shape it as best you can into an image of Jesus Christ. You have 60 seconds. Ready? Go.

Call time after 60 seconds, and have each person show off his or her sculpture. Obviously, because the clay was frozen, most of these sculptures will simply look like lumps of clay. Affirm each person for his or her attempt without acknowledging that the clay was frozen and that the sculptures are mostly disappointing replicas of Jesus. After everyone has had an opportunity to show a sculpture, have group members find a partner to discuss these questions:

> *What was your initial reaction when you tried to mold an image of Christ out of your clay?*

> *What steps might have been taken to help you be more successful in your attempt to replicate Jesus in the clay?*

Have pairs read Romans 8:29 and continue their discussions by responding to these questions:

> *How does it make you feel to know that God wants to mold you, like clay, into the image of Jesus Christ?*

> *What makes it difficult for you to become more like Jesus in the way you live and think and act in your daily life?*

> *What steps might you take to help you better cooperate with God as he molds you into the image of his Son?*

When partners are ready, ask for a volunteer from each pair to share the results of their discussions with the whole group.

Wrap up this learning activity by saying:

We have been chosen to become like Christ. *Like the frozen clay we handled earlier, we can fight God's shaping influence on us. Or we can warm our hearts and souls and make ourselves people who respond willingly to God's loving touch in our lives.*

Continue your small-group or Sunday School lesson as planned.

Tip

If modeling clay is difficult to obtain, you may consider substituting Play-Doh, although it may take a little longer to freeze Play-Doh.

Also, if you have more than 12 people in your group or if you are running short on modeling clay, have learners do this activity in pairs or trios to cut down on the amount of clay you'll need.

42

If I Had a Servant

Risk Rating: Low

Scripture: Romans 12:13

Key Verse: "When God's people are in need, be ready to help them" (Romans 12:13a).

Theme: Serving

Point: We are called to serve, and when we all do that, everyone reaps the benefits.

Synopsis: Learners will list their preferences for a servant.

Supplies: Two index cards and a pencil for each participant and a hat

Preparation: Acquire your supplies ahead of time, and pray for God to bless your teaching efforts today.

Begin this small-group or Sunday school activity by distributing two index cards and a pencil to everyone. On the first index card, have group members finish these five sentences:

• *If I had a servant, the first thing I'd stop doing is…*

• *If I had a servant, a job that would get done at my home that hasn't been done in ages is…*

• *If I had a servant, it would give me time to…*

• *If I had a servant, the thing that might make me uncomfortable would be…*

• *If I had a servant, the way my life would change most would be…*

When participants have finished writing their thoughts in response to these sentence starters, collect all the index cards in a hat. One by one, pull out the cards and read some of the more interesting responses.

When you're ready, tell group members to pull out the second index card and complete these sentences on it:

- *If I were a servant, the first thing I'd stop doing is…*
- *If I were a servant, a job that would get done at my home that hasn't been done in ages is…*
- *If I were a servant, it would give me time to…*
- *If I were a servant, the thing that might make me uncomfortable would be…*
- *If I were a servant, the way my life would change most would be…*

> **Tip**
>
> If your group members are comfortable with each other, it might be fun to have people try to guess which responses go with which person in your group when reading the index cards.

Afterward, collect these cards as well, and take turns reading some of the responses on them to the group at large. Then have everyone find a partner nearby and read Romans 12:13 together. Then ask pairs to discuss these questions:

- *In your opinion, which is more likely to make a lasting impact: having a servant or being a servant?*
- *Why do you suppose Romans 12:13 challenges us to serve each other during times of need?*
- *How do we serve each other best in times of need? List at least five specific ways.*
- *What can we do to help each other become reliable servants?*

Say: *As Romans 12:13 reminds us, **we are called to serve, and when we all do that, everyone reaps the benefits.***

Continue your lesson as planned.

43

Circle Out, Circle In

Risk Rating: Medium

Scripture: Romans 12:15-20

Key Verse: "Do all that you can to live in peace with everyone" (Romans 12:18).

Theme: Reconciliation

Point: We're meant to be together.

Synopsis: Learners will experience separation and reconciliation.

Supplies: None

Preparation: Pray for God to bless your teaching efforts today.

Begin this learning activity by reading aloud Romans 12:15-20. Ask for a few people from your small group or Sunday school class to volunteer their responses to these questions:

• *Why do you suppose the Apostle Paul felt it was important to give this advice to the Romans?*

• *Why do you think this Scripture passage continues to be good advice for Christians today?*

Next, have everyone in your small group or Sunday school class form a circle. This can be done in one large group if the room permits; otherwise, form groups of six to eight people, and have each group form a circle somewhere in the room. Have group members place their arms around each other as you say:

Being a part of a group can be wonderful because we can enjoy feelings of togetherness and support. But it doesn't always work that way.

Pause for a moment, then continue:

Sometimes we separate ourselves from each other and can't enjoy the kind of love that is described in Romans 12:15-20. (Pause for a short time.)

If you have been part of a group and have ever let that group down, I'd like you to drop your arms to your sides. (Pause.)

Sometimes we say things that are harmful to other people and disrupt the harmony of the group. (Short pause.)

I'd like anyone who's ever said something harmful—either intentionally or unintentionally—to another member of a group to take a step backward. (Pause.)

Often we exclude others from our group. (Short pause.)

If anyone has ever excluded another person from a group or made someone feel left out—either intentionally or unintentionally—please take a step backward. (Pause.)

Sometimes we say things that aren't true. We deny making a mistake, or we're just afraid to admit something to others. (Short pause.)

If this has ever happened to you, I'd like you to turn and face away from the center of the circle. (Pause.)

Sometimes we pretend not to see the needs of others. (Short pause.)

If there have been times you've ignored the needs of others, I'd like you to close your eyes and keep them closed. (Pause.)

As Romans 12:15-20 makes clear, **we're meant to be together,** *yet at times our actions keep us apart.* (Short pause.)

If you've ever helped someone with a need, I'd like you to turn around. (Pause.)

It's important to listen to people. (Short pause.)

If you've ever taken the time to listen to a friend who had a problem, I'd like you to take one step in. (Pause.)

We build people up when we welcome them and make them feel included. (Short pause.)

If you've ever made someone feel welcome and a part of things, open your eyes. (Pause.)

Confession to one another can tear down walls. (Short pause.)

If you've ever admitted that you failed someone, even if it was hard to do, take another step in. (Pause.)

God asks us to forgive one another. (Short pause.)

If you've ever forgiven someone, place your arms around the people beside you.

Pause once more and suggest that learners take advantage of the moment to give each other a group hug. Then have everyone find a partner to discuss these questions:

Tip

• How did you feel during the first half of this experience? Explain.

• How did your feelings change during the second half of the experience?

• How was this experience like what happens in our relationships with others?

• What can we learn from this experience to help us better follow God's instructions in Romans 12:15-20?

Have pairs take turns sharing insights from their discussions with the larger group. Then continue your lesson as planned.

If members of your small group or Sunday school class seem reluctant to volunteer their thoughts during large-group discussions, try one of these techniques to encourage greater participation:

• Designate the person wearing the most red (or the person born closest to today, the person who lives closest to your church, and so on) in each pair as that twosome's spokesperson whose duty it is to record and share insights from partner discussions.

• Tell partners they are a "Finish Each Other's Sentences" pair. Then, during report-back time, have one partner begin a sentence that reveals something they discussed, and have the second partner finish the sentence.

• Have pairs join with another group (to form groups of four), and then have a less shy representative from the newly-formed foursome report results of discussions for both pairs in the group.

Dirty Hands

Risk Rating: Medium

Scripture: 1 Corinthians 6:9-11

Key Verse: "You were cleansed" (1 Corinthians 6:11b).

Theme: Salvation

Point: We are all stained by sin.

Synopsis: Learners will see a visual representation of sin.

Supplies: Newspapers and several damp white towels

Preparation: Acquire your supplies ahead of time, and pray for God to bless your teaching efforts today.

At the appropriate time during your lesson, have learners form pairs with others in the group with whom they feel comfortable. Give each pair a section of newspaper. Have one partner hold the newspaper on the floor while the other partner drags his or her hands, palms down, across it several times. Then have partners switch roles and repeat the process. The result should be that both partners' hands are stained with newsprint.

Prompt group members to examine their hands and to discuss these questions with their partners:

• *How is staining your hands with newspaper ink like getting involved in sin?*

• *How is it like or unlike sin's real effect on us?*

Next read aloud 1 Corinthians 6:9-10. Ask group members to quietly reflect on their own lives and to consider the times they've fallen short of God's standards in their attitudes or actions. Then say:

*We may not feel that we are outwardly guilty of the individual wrongs listed in 1 Corinthians 6:9-10, but **we are all stained by sin** and guilty* *of falling short of God's standards in many, many ways. Left to our own devices, we would be forever stained by the sin that so often overwhelms our lives. However, we haven't been left to our own devices. Listen to what the rest of this Scripture says.*

Read aloud 1 Corinthians 6:11, with special emphasis on the last half of that verse. Then hold up the damp white towels. Say:

This towel represents how "you were made right with God by calling on the name of the Lord Jesus Christ and by the Spirit of our God."

Pass the towels to your group members, and allow them to wipe their hands clean with the towels. When everyone is finished, say:

We are all stained by sin, *but we can take heart in knowing that Jesus is ready, willing, and able to wash our sins away.*

Then continue your lesson as planned.

Lesson From a Leaf

Risk Rating: Low

Scripture: 1 Corinthians 12:1-11

Key Verse: "A spiritual gift is given to each of us" (1 Corinthians 12:7a).

Theme: Spiritual Gifts

Point: God has given you unique gifts.

Synopsis: Learners will examine a leaf as an example of God's gifting ability.

Supplies: Leaves from several trees and plants—enough for each person to have one

Preparation: Acquire your supplies ahead of time, and pray for God to bless your teaching efforts today.

At the appropriate time during your small-group or Sunday school lesson, distribute one leaf to each person in your group. Ask a volunteer to read 1 Corinthians 12:1-11 aloud for the rest of the group. Then say:

Now please turn your attention to the leaf I've given you. (Pause.)
Study it for a moment. (Pause.)
Look at its delicate veins. (Pause.)
Notice the shades of color on the leaf. (Pause.)
Examine the texture of your leaf. (Pause.)
Turn it over and note any interesting aspects of its shape. (Pause.)

Summarize the experience by saying:

The leaf in your hand is different from any other leaf in the world. In fact, it is unique. God attends to all the intricate details of its design. And if you hadn't taken the time to examine and explore it, the leaf would have probably

gone unobserved and unappreciated.

In a way, you are a lot like that leaf. You have been carefully created by God himself. And as 1 Corinthians 12:1-11 tells us, **God has given you unique gifts.** *God attended to all the intricate details of your design, including your gifts. Can you imagine the loss if you were to allow God's gifts in you to go unexamined and unappreciated?*

Pause for a moment to let group members reflect on your statements. Then suggest that everyone take his or her leaf home as a reminder of the gifts of God that reside within. Afterward, continue your lesson as planned.

A Rose by Any Other Name

Risk Rating: Low

Scripture: 2 Corinthians 2:15-17

Key Verse: "Our lives are a Christ-like fragrance rising up to God" (2 Corinthians 2:15a).

Theme: Sharing Faith

Point: We are God's perfume to the world.

Synopsis: Learners will pass a rose through the group and then compare themselves to the rose.

Supplies: A red rose with thorns

Preparation: Acquire your supplies ahead of time, and pray for God to bless your teaching efforts today.

At the appropriate time during your lesson, show your small group or Sunday school class the rose that you brought to the meeting. Ask learners to pass the rose from one person to another, pausing briefly to examine it, until it has passed through the hands of everyone in the room.

Ask group members to volunteer their responses to these questions:

• *What did you notice about this rose as it passed through your hands?*

• *Was your impression of the rose positive or negative? Why?*

• *Why do you suppose the same flower can leave different impressions on us?*

• *How many of you took a second to smell the rose? Why did you do—or not do—that?*

Have group members find a partner and read 2 Corinthians 2:15-17 in their pairs. Then have pairs discuss these questions:

• *In what ways were our descriptions of the rose similar to the way*

2 Corinthians 2:15–17 describes us?

• Why do you suppose the Apostle Paul chose to describe us as a "fragrance" in the world?

• What is our responsibility when spreading the fragrance of Jesus' love into the world?

• How does a rose decide when to perfume its surroundings? What implications might that have for us as Christians who spread God's perfume into the world?

Have pairs take turns sharing insights from their discussions with the larger group. Then say:

We are God's perfume to the world. *Some love the fragrance we bring; others are offended or uninterested in it. But like the rose, we bring a unique aspect of God's beauty simply by living our Christian lives out in the open.*

Continue with your lesson as planned.

> **Tip**
>
> If your group is more than 12 people, you may want to supply additional roses and have groups of 12 (or so) pass each rose around. This will save some time in your overall meeting.

Chair Concerns

Risk Rating: Medium

Scripture: Galatians 5:14-15

Key Verse: "Beware of destroying one another" (Galatians 5:15b).

Theme: Conflict

Point: God can help us overcome obstacles to conflict resolution.

Synopsis: Learners will try to overcome obstacles in communication as a means to spark discussion about overcoming obstacles in conflict resolution.

Supplies: None

Preparation: Pray for God to bless your teaching efforts today.

Form pairs, and have each pair find a place to sit together in the room. Have partners designate one person in each pair as A and the other person as B.

Call all the B's into a huddle around you. Without letting the A's hear you, say to the B's:

Your goal for the next few minutes is to convince your partner to give you his or her seat. However, there is an obstacle you have to overcome. The only method of communication you can use is facial expressions. That means once you return to your partner, you must freeze every part of your body except your face. No head bobbing, no nodding or shaking your head, no arm motions or other body language—nothing. All you can do is move your face: your nose, eyebrows, forehead, and so on. You may move your mouth, but you may not mouth any words. Only when you are able to convince your partner to give you the seat will you be allowed to move again.

Make sure everyone understands the rules, then give the B's two minutes to try to overcome their communication obstacle and gain their partners' seats. Call time after two minutes. Then gather the whole group into a circle and explain to the A's what was going on.

Have everyone stand as you ask the following questions. When one person shares an answer, anyone who agrees with that answer and has nothing more to add may sit down. When everyone is seated, ask everyone to stand again as you ask the next question and repeat the process. Ask:

• *What were you feeling and thinking during this activity?*

• *What made it easy or difficult for you to overcome the obstacle to communication imposed on you during this activity?*

• *What makes it easy or difficult for you to overcome obstacles when you face conflict in your relationships?*

Have a volunteer read Galatians 5:14-15 aloud. Ask:

• *How would you summarize the message the Apostle Paul is trying to communicate in this passage of Scripture?*

• *How might and following the instructions of Galatians 5:14-15 help us to overcome conflicts in our relationships?*

• *What are specific things we can do in the way we communicate that will help us overcome obstacles to conflict resolution?*

Say: **God can help us overcome obstacles to conflict resolution** *when we let our relationships be governed by the message of Galatians 5:14-15.*

Wrap up this activity with this short affirmation exercise. Have group members turn to their right or left to form pairs, and have partners face each other. Say:

To communicate joy that your partner is a part of our group, smile at each other. (Pause as group members respond.) *To communicate acceptance of your partner, nod approvingly to each other.* (Pause.) *To communicate God's love to your partner, shake hands warmly or hug each other right now.* (Pause.)

Then continue your lesson as planned.

48

Passing Grade

Risk Rating: Low

Scripture: Ephesians 2:1-10

Key Verse: "God is so rich in mercy" (Ephesians 2:4a).

Theme: Grace

Point: God is so rich in mercy that he has made a way to heaven for us even though we don't deserve it.

Synopsis: Learners will grade themselves and then receive a "grade" from God.

Supplies: Enough "report cards" (as described below) for everyone in your group to have one of each kind. You'll also need pencils and a wastebasket.

Preparation: Before your meeting, prepare report cards by folding sheets of paper in half and writing "Report Card" on the front of each one. Then take half of the report cards and write "A+" inside the fold. Leave the inside of the other report cards blank. Prepare one of each kind of card for each participant.

Use this experience to help participants understand the true nature of God's grace. This exercise is particularly meaningful for newer Christians. Begin by saying:

Let's try an exercise in "sanctified imagination." Imagine for a moment that we're all standing before God at the pearly gates of heaven. We want to get into heaven, but God has halted us and is asking for our report cards.

At this point, distribute the blank report cards and pencils and say:

Think back on your life. If you had to give yourself an honest "grade" that assessed how well you have lived out the Christian life, what would that grade be? On the inside fold of your report card, write the grade you think you would deserve. You won't be showing your grade to anyone else.

Give participants a moment to reflect and write their responses.

Next, take a wastebasket and the pre-graded (A+) report cards and begin moving toward each individual in your group. As you approach each person, take the report card in his or her hand and—without looking at the grade—crumple it and drop it in the wastebasket. Then give that person one of the A+ report cards. Be sure that everyone in the group receives one of the new A+ report cards. After everyone has looked at his or her new report card, say:

The report cards that we threw into that wastebasket would have kept each one of us out of heaven. We most certainly would have been expelled. After all, how many of us realistically deserve an A+ from God? However, the Bible makes it clear that the only grade that will get us into heaven is the A+ given by God. And he gives it to us freely through Jesus Christ—that's the way his grace works! Listen to what the Scripture says...

Read Ephesians 2:1-10 aloud, with emphasis on verses 8 and 9. Then say: **God is so rich in mercy that he has made a way to heaven for us even though we don't deserve it.**

Continue your lesson as planned.

Heavy Burdens

Risk Rating: Medium

Scripture: Colossians 3:13

Key Verse: "Make allowance for each other's faults" (Colossians 3:13a).

Theme: Relationships

Point: God forgave us, so we can forgive others.

Synopsis: Learners will hold onto heavy burdens as a physical representation of unforgiveness in a relationship.

Supplies: Five to 10 books—such as hymnals—for each participant

Preparation: Acquire your supplies ahead of time. Before your small-group or Sunday school gathering, place the large supply of books in an easily accessible place in your meeting room. Don't forget to pray for God to bless your teaching efforts today.

Begin this portion of your small-group or Sunday school lesson by saying:

Today we're going to focus on a key ingredient for developing healthy relationships with family, friends, co-workers, and others: a commitment to forgive.

Have adults stand around the supply of books you set up prior to the meeting.

Read the following sentences one at a time, allowing time for everyone to perform the actions described. Participants should collect new books for each situation described, with the result being that each person will likely end up holding several books.

• *Pick up and hold one book for each time a friend or family member hurt you with words or actions in the past week.*

• *Pick up and hold one book for each time you've hurt a friend or family member with your words or actions in the past week.*

• *Pick up and hold one book for each time a friend or family member has lied to you or somehow deceived you in the past week.*

• *Pick up and hold one book for each time you've lied to or misled a friend or family member in the past week.*

• *Pick up and hold one book for each time a friend or family member has treated you disrespectfully in the past week.*

• *Pick up and hold one book for each time you've treated a friend or family member disrespectfully in the past week.*

• *Pick up and hold one book for each time you felt that a friend or family member betrayed your trust in the past week.*

• *Pick up and hold one book for each time a friend or family member felt that you betrayed his or her trust in the past week.*

• *Pick up and hold one book for each time you and a friend or family member got into an argument in the past week.*

• *Pick up and hold one book for each time you and a friend or family member spoke unkindly to each other in the past week.*

• *Pick up and hold one book for each time a friend or family member made you angry at him or her in the past week.*

Tip

If you're having trouble gathering enough books for each person in your group to do this activity individually, consider one of the following options:

• If your group has 10 or fewer members, you might arrange to have your small group or Sunday school class meet at a local library or bookstore.

• You might ask each group member to bring 10 books to your meeting.

• Depending on your local library's loaning policy, you and a few friends might try to check out enough books from the library for this activity.

• If all else fails, have group members work in pairs or trios as you conduct this learning activity. If you use this option, have partners take turns holding the pile of books and adding to it.

Tell group members to continue holding their books and to find a partner to form pairs. Some people may be carrying a lot of books, while others may have only a few. Tell group members to hold the books in their laps while they discuss the following questions:

• *What does this activity reveal to us about our need for forgiveness in our relationships with others?*

• *How is the burden of carrying these books like the burden we carry when we let unforgiveness reign in our relationships?*

Have group members set their books in the center of the room and then return to their seats empty-handed. Read Colossians 3:13 aloud. Then ask:

• *What's it like to be rid of those books?*

• *How is this similar to, or different from, the feeling we have when we are able to forgive or be forgiven?*

• *Why do you suppose the Apostle Paul felt it was important to include the words of Colossians 3:13 in this letter?*

• *How might your life be different if you obeyed the words in Colossians 3:13 each of the next seven days? What can you do to help make that happen?*

Wrap up this experience by saying:

The point of this experience is very simple to say, but sometimes hard to live. **God forgave us, so we can forgive others.** *Let's pray this week for God to help us to accomplish his forgiveness in our relationships with others.*

Tip

If you have more than 10 people in your small group or Sunday school class, you may want to form groups of 10 or fewer and give each group its own supply of books for this activity.

Tip

If your group runs out of books before going through the complete list of statements, simply end your reading of the "Pick up and hold a book..." sentences at that point and move on to the next portion of the activity.

50

What's in Your Wallet?

Risk Rating: Medium

Scripture: Colossians 3:17

Key Verse: "And whatever you do or say, do it as a representative of the Lord Jesus" (Colossians 3:17a).

Theme: Christ-likeness

Point: The way we live, act, and talk reveals something about Whose we are.

Synopsis: Learners will reveal the contents of their wallets as a springboard for a discussion on Christ-like living.

Supplies: None

Preparation: Pray for God to bless your teaching efforts today.

At the appropriate time during your small-group or Sunday school lesson, have learners form groups of no more than three people. If possible, encourage people to join a group with at least one person they don't know well.

After everyone has formed a trio, say:

Today we're going to learn a bit more about each other through a simple exercise. Beginning with the person in your group who's been at our church the longest, pull at least six different items from your pockets, purse, or wallet for all of your partners to see. Coins or multiples of any other objects count as only one item. Display the items in front of you, but don't tell anyone anything about them.

Allow people to select items they feel comfortable showing to others. Suggest things such as keys, photographs, candy wrappers, ticket stubs, and driver's licenses. Then have people in each trio spend a few minutes examining the items their partners have displayed. If necessary, remind the owners of the items not to say anything about the things they've displayed.

After a few moments, have group members tell each other what they might assume about their partners based only on the items they've shown from their pockets, purses, and wallets. For example, someone might say, "You seem to be interested in sports because you have a ticket to a basketball game," or "You're very proud of your family because you carry lots of their pictures." Tell people to neither confirm nor deny assumptions during this time.

> **Tip**
>
> If your small group or Sunday school class has five or fewer participants, then there's no need to form groups of three. Simply conduct the activity with your whole group.

Allow about five minutes for people to share their thoughts. Afterward, ask participants to share with their partners which assumptions were accurate and which were not. Then ask trios to discuss the following questions with their partners:

• *What did you learn about one another through this exercise?*

• *How did it feel to see yourself accurately represented by the contents of your pockets, purse, or wallet? to see yourself inaccurately represented?*

• *What clues about who you are do you display—consciously or unconsciously—when you go about your normal daily life?*

Ask volunteers to share their trios' insights with the whole group. Then say:

*Just as tokens from our wallets reveal something about who we are, **the way we live, act, and talk reveals something about Whose we are.***

Read Colossians 3:17 aloud, and ask:

• *In what ways do we best display Christ to others as we go about our normal daily lives?*

• *What happens when a Christian's life negatively represents Christ? What should we do in that situation?*

• *What would help you be a better reflection of Christ during the upcoming week?*

After discussion, continue your lesson as planned.

51

Strange Behavior

Risk Rating: Medium

Scripture: 1 Thessalonians 4:1

Key Verse: "Live in a way that pleases God" (1 Thessalonians 4:1b).

Theme: Right Living

Point: The Christian life often seems absurd to those outside the faith.

Synopsis: Learners will act out strange behavior as an example of the way Christian standards are viewed by the non-Christian world.

Supplies: None

Preparation: Pray for God to bless your teaching efforts today.

At the appropriate time in your small-group or Sunday school lesson, have everyone gather and sit in a circle. Then say:

Before we go any further in this lesson, I'd like to ask each of you to do several things that may seem, well, unusual. Ready? Here we go.

• *First, turn and face away from me.* (Pause.)

• *Stick out your tongue and practice making a silly face.* (Pause.)

• *Now wave your right hand in the air.* (Pause.)

• *Now put your right hand down and show off your silly face to your neighbor.* (Pause.)

• *Now stand tall and wave your hands high in the air.* (Pause.)

• *Now try to steal someone else's seat.* (Pause.)

• *Now try to convince your neighbor to give you money. See who can collect the most money without stealing it!*

Allow a minute for people to try to collect money; then just for fun see if anyone was successful. Afterward, ask group members to volunteer their responses to these questions:

• *What went through your mind as you saw everyone following my strange instructions?*

• *How did you react when I gave each new instruction?*

• *How was your reaction influenced by others in the group?*

Say:

My off-the-wall instructions created a low-risk dilemma for you to respond to, but God's instructions for the way we are to live often cause dilemmas that pose a much higher risk.

Ask a volunteer to read 1 Thessalonians 4:1 aloud. Then ask:

• *What's risky about living life in a way that pleases God?*

• *Why do people outside the Christian faith often view the Christian lifestyle as strange or unnatural?*

• *What do you think it means to truly live out a strange, risky life that pleases God?*

Wrap up this experience by saying:

The Christian life often seems absurd to those outside the faith. *But only when we live according to the guidelines of 1 Thessalonians 4:1 can we truly experience the abundant life of God.*

52

Mr. Holland's Opus

Risk Rating: Low

Scripture: 1 Thessalonians 5:12-13

Key Verse: "Honor those who are your leaders in the Lord's work" (1 Thessalonians 5:12b).

Theme: Honoring Leaders

Point: God has blessed us with Christian leaders in our church.

Synopsis: Learners will view and discuss a clip from the film *Mr. Holland's Opus.*

Supplies: A DVD version of the 1996 film *Mr. Holland's Opus* (rated PG, starring Richard Dreyfuss) and the ability to show a clip from this DVD

Preparation: Acquire your supplies ahead of time, and pray for God to bless your teaching efforts today. The film clip for this experience is located in tracks 23 and 24 on the DVD, beginning about two hours and six minutes from the start of the movie. This clip runs from time counter point 2:06:08 (the beginning of track 23) through 2:13:15 (about midway through track 24). Please be sure to preview this clip to make sure its content is appropriate for your group.

At the appropriate time during your small-group or Sunday school lesson, introduce the DVD clip from *Mr. Holland's Opus* by saying:

In 1996 Richard Dreyfuss starred in the film Mr. Holland's Opus, *a movie about the life and work of an obscure high school music teacher. I'd like*

for us to watch a short scene from that film today.

Richard Dreyfuss plays Glenn Holland, a young musician and composer who takes what he thinks will be a short-term job teaching music to students. Thirty years later, he is still teaching. When budget cuts threaten the music program at his school near the end of Glenn Holland's career, his past and present students gather in his honor. Let's watch what happens next...

Show the clip from the movie. At the end of the clip, pause for a moment to allow it to sink in, then ask group members to reflect on these questions:

• *What's your initial reaction to this clip?*

• *If we were to brainstorm a list of the specific ways Mr. Holland's students honored him for his influence in their lives, what might be on that list?*

Read aloud 1 Thessalonians 5:12-13. Ask:

• *What might happen if we treated our pastors and other church leaders with the same honor and gratitude that Mr. Holland's students showed to him?*

• *What keeps us from continually following the advice of 1 Thessalonians 5:12-13?*

• *If we were to brainstorm a list of the specific ways we could honor our church leaders this week for their influence in our lives, what might be on that list?*

> **Tip**
>
> In general, federal copyright laws do not allow you to use videos or DVDs (even ones you own) for any purpose other than home viewing. Though some exceptions allow for the use of short segments of copyrighted material for educational purposes, it's best to be on the safe side. Your church can obtain a license from Christian Video Licensing for a small fee. Just visit www.cvli.org or call 1-888-771-2854 for more information. When using a movie that is not covered by the license, we recommend directly contacting the movie studio to seek permission to use the clip.

Wrap up this experience by saying: ***God has blessed us with Christian leaders in our church.*** *Let's be a blessing to them in return.*

Then continue your lesson as planned.

53

Monsters!

Risk Rating: Medium

Scripture: 2 Timothy 1:7

Key Verse: "God has not given us a spirit of fear" (2 Timothy 1:7a).

Theme: Fear

Point: God's Holy Spirit can help us overcome all fears.

Synopsis: Learners will listen to a reading of a classic picture book and then discuss it in light of Scripture.

Supplies: A copy of the classic Sesame Street picture book *The Monster at the End of This Book* (Little Golden Books)

Preparation: Acquire your supplies ahead of time, and pray for God to bless your teaching efforts today. Most libraries will have a copy of *The Monster at the End of This Book*. You should also be able to find this book at most bookstores.

Tell participants that for the next few minutes you'd like to help them remember what it was like to be a child. Tell everyone that you'll be reading aloud the classic children's book *The Monster at the End of This Book: Starring Lovable, Furry Old Grover*, and that, yes, you'll be doing the silly voices that go along with reading a kids' book.

When everyone is settled in and prepared for this temporary return to childhood, real aloud *The Monster at the End of This Book*. In this entertaining little story, Sesame Street Muppet Grover speaks directly to the reader about his fear of meeting a monster hidden on the last page of the book. The bulk of the book, then, is Grover trying to find creative ways to keep the reader from turning pages—thus allowing him to avoid meeting the monster at the end. When the reader finally gets to the last page, he or she discovers—along with the Muppet narrator—that Grover himself is the "monster" at the end of the book and that there was no reason to be afraid after all.

As you read, be sure to play up the suspense of the story, and to allow everyone a chance to view the delightful illustrations on each page.

After reading the story, have everyone in your small group number off from one to two. Have all the Ones gather together to discuss these questions:

• *What kinds of physical, spiritual, or emotional "monsters" cause people to feel fearful in real life?*

• *What were Grover's tactics for dealing with his fear of monsters? What tactics do people typically use to deal with fear?*

• *In what ways was Grover his own worst enemy in this situation?*

• *What can we learn from Grover's experience about dealing with fear in our own lives?*

> **Tip**
>
> Some adults may feel jaded about having a child's book read to them in an adult group. The key to making this work, then, will be for you to lead by example—to read with enthusiasm and to demonstrate that it's OK for adults to embrace a childlike moment. If you lead in this way, you'll make it safe for your group members to follow you—and thus to benefit from the deep, adult-focused insights in the discussion that follows the reading.

Have all the Twos gather as well. Instruct them to read 2 Timothy 1:7 and to discuss these questions:

• *Would you say that fear is a positive, negative, or neutral emotion? Explain your answer.*

• *What is God's responsibility when we are afraid?*

• *How does faith in Christ combat fear? Be specific.*

• *At some point in the coming week, each of us is going to feel some measure of fear even if it's in the form of worry, stress, or anxiety. With 2 Timothy 1:7 in mind, what advice would you like to give yourself about that upcoming situation?*

After groups have had time to discuss their assigned questions, have each of the Ones find a Two and form a pair. Then have everyone take turns reporting the results of the previous group's discussion to his or her new partner. Afterward, invite volunteers from the group at large to share any insights gained from their discussions.

Wrap up this activity by saying:

Fear is a normal part of the human experience, but the lesson we can learn from Grover and from 2 Timothy 1:7 is this: Fear need never control nor overwhelm us. **God's Holy Spirit can help us overcome all fears.**

54

Puzzler

Risk Rating: Medium

Scripture: 2 Timothy 3:16-17

Key Verse: "All Scripture is inspired by God" (2 Timothy 3:16a).

Theme: The Bible

Point: God's Word has great value in our lives.

Synopsis: Learners will attempt to piece together incomplete puzzles in preparation for a discussion of the Bible.

Supplies: Four puzzles with 25 to 50 pieces each

Preparation: Acquire your supplies ahead of time. Take pieces from each puzzle and mix them up in the other puzzles. For example, you might remove 10 pieces from one puzzle and place some of them in two or three of the other puzzles. Don't place pieces of one puzzle in *every* puzzle, just in some of them. When you're finished, you should have puzzles that can only be completed if groups get pieces from each other. Pray for God to bless your teaching efforts today.

At the appropriate time during your small-group or Sunday school lesson, form four groups (a group can be one person). Give each group one of the mixed-up puzzles to put together. Don't tell anyone that the puzzles have been mixed up.

People will soon discover that they have parts of other groups' puzzles and are missing some of their own. When this happens, tell groups that they may send out members one at a time to ask for a puzzle piece from another group. Participants must describe the kind of puzzle piece they want, but they may not point to or pick up any puzzle piece. Based on their descriptions, the other group may give the requesting person a puzzle piece.

Continue until all the puzzles are completed. Then have people discuss the following questions within their groups. After discussing each question, have volunteers share their groups' insights with the rest of the small group or Sunday school class. Encourage a variety of responses before moving on. Ask:

• *What was it like to discover you didn't have all the pieces of your puzzle?*

• *How is that like the way you feel when you realize you don't have all the pieces for answering an important question in life?*

• *In what ways was your group's search for puzzle pieces like the way we search the Bible for answers in our lives? like the way we uncover answers to puzzling questions in the pages of Scripture?*

Say: **God's Word has great value in our lives.** *Listen to how the Apostle Paul described that.*

Have someone in each group read aloud 2 Timothy 3:16-17 for the rest of the people on his or her team. Then ask groups to continue their discussions with these questions:

• *What does this Scripture say the Bible is good for? When have you seen that to be true in your own life?*

• *What happens when we neglect the benefits of the Bible that are described in this passage?*

• *When is the Bible misused in ways that corrupt the benefits listed in 2 Timothy 3:16-17?*

• *What strategies can we employ to help us pursue the benefits of the Bible in our lives and avoid misuse and neglect of Scripture at the same time?*

After discussions, continue your lesson as planned.

55

Christianity Isn't for Wimps

Risk Rating: Low

Scripture: 2 Timothy 4:5

Key Verse: "Don't be afraid of suffering for the Lord" (2 Timothy 4:5b).

Theme: Suffering

Point: We can expect to suffer for our belief in Jesus Christ.

Synopsis: Learners will search the room for representations of suffering.

Supplies: Paper and pencils

Preparation: Acquire your supplies ahead of time, and ask God to bless your teaching efforts today.

At an opportune time during your lesson, have everyone in your small group or Sunday school class pause to conduct a search within your meeting room. Tell learners to search for things that represent suffering that occurs in a normal Christian's life. For instance, a broken pencil might represent poor health, a crumpled paper might represent antagonism from non-Christians, a coin might represent financial stress, a plant might represent dry and lonely times, and so on. Tell group members they can each gather as many items as they want, but each person must select at least one thing that represents suffering.

After everyone has gathered at least one item, have group members explain their items and the type of suffering they represent. On a sheet of paper, list the types of suffering that are mentioned so you can discuss them later.

When everyone has shared, ask group members to volunteer their responses to these questions:

*   *How many of the things we mentioned are simply a part of life, and how many are brought about because of our belief in Jesus Christ?*
*   *What kinds of thoughts go through our minds when we find ourselves suffering unexpectedly? What kinds of fears?*

Have a volunteer read 2 Timothy 4:5 aloud. Have group members find a partner, and distribute a sheet of paper and a pencil to each pair. Then ask pairs to summarize this verse in their own words and in one sentence. Have several pairs share their summaries. Then ask:

*   *Does this passage of Scripture change the way you look at the representations of suffering we shared earlier? Why or why not?*
*   *What do you think it takes to "keep a clear mind" when we're suffering?*
*   *Why do you suppose God allows his children to suffer when they are working for the Lord?*
*   *What can we do this week to help each other face suffering with the same attitude described in 2 Timothy 4:5?*

Wrap up this activity by saying:

We can expect to suffer for belief in Jesus Christ—*but we don't have to be overwhelmed by that suffering. By God's grace, we can live out 2 Timothy 4:5, and we can help our Christian brothers and sisters to do the same.*

make your message stick...on holidays and special occasions

In this section you'll find 15 creative activities to use in celebration of holidays and special occasions. As before, the ideas here vary in style and content, but all conform to the following standards:

• They are drawn from specific Scripture passages and themes.

• They somehow involve everyone in the group in the learning experience.

• They are appropriate for groups of just about any size, from three to 3,000 people.

• They can be done with few (or no) props and simple preparation.

One thing that's different about this section is that the ideas can be used in a variety of settings—from the pulpit, in small groups, in Sunday school classes, in staff meetings, and so on. We've indicated the most likely setting for each idea in parentheses under the title, but feel free to adapt an activity to any setting in which you feel it is relevant.

As with other activities in this book, debriefing and partner discussions are often included. If that element is included in an idea that we expect you'll use from the pulpit, we've automatically given it a medium-risk rating. And, as before, if we expect you to use that idea in a setting other than a formal sermon, we've lowered the risk rating.

Thanks for being willing to celebrate the power of God to change the world!

56

Baby Powder and the Holy Child

Risk Rating: Medium

Scripture: Romans 1:2-3; 15:8-13

Key Verse: "Remember that Christ came as a servant" (Romans 15:8a).

Theme: Christmas

Point: When we celebrate Jesus' birth, we celebrate more than just another holiday.

Synopsis: (for use from the pulpit) Audience members will examine a fragrant piece of fabric to prompt contemplation of Jesus' humanity and divinity.

Supplies: One-inch strips of fabric (old receiving blankets torn into strips work well for this), baby powder, and a box

Preparation: Acquire your supplies ahead of time, and pray for God to bless your teaching efforts today. Place the strips of cloth in a box. So that the smell of the powder stays fresh, sprinkle baby powder over the strips just before worshippers arrive.

As congregation members enter, ask each person to take one of the strips of cloth and to hold it throughout the service.

As a call to worship, read aloud Romans 1:2-3 and 15:8-13. These verses emphasize Jesus' humanity ("In his earthly life, he was born into King David's family line"), his humility ("Christ came as a servant"), and his mercy toward Jew and Gentile alike ("Rejoice with his people, you Gentiles"). Then begin teaching about the stunning truth of Christ's incarnation into our world. Like these Scriptures, emphasize Jesus' deity and humanity, his humility, and his sacrificial service to all the peoples of the world. Then, at an appropriate time during your sermon, say:

When we celebrate Jesus' birth, we celebrate more than just another holiday. *It is a commemoration of the moment when God gave up his right to give us everything we deserved and instead gave us everything we didn't deserve. Let's take a moment now to meditate on the significance of that divine action. Take the piece of fabric you received when you entered the auditorium today. Hold that fabric up to your face and feel its softness.*

Pause as congregation members respond. Then say:

Now smell your cloth. Think about the memories that its touch and fragrance elicit.

Pause; then say:

Now turn to someone nearby and take a moment to share some of the memories that have come to you from touching and smelling the cloth.

> **Tip**
>
> Although rare, it is possible that some in your congregation might be allergic to baby powder. As a precaution, be sure to include a small sign on your box indicating that the cloth strips inside contain baby powder and warning anyone with allergies to that kind of powder not to take a cloth.

Allow congregation members a few minutes to share memories; then call everyone's attention back to you and say:

It's amazing to think Romans 1:3 is true, that God's only Son came to earth as a man. It's even more astounding that he came into the world as Romans 15:8 tells us he did: as a servant. But perhaps the greatest mystery of all time is that this God–Man and Servant–King chose to make his entry into our existence as a tiny baby—weak, vulnerable, and dependent on a human mother and father. Imagine what it might have been like to feed baby Jesus, to rock the Christ child to sleep in your arms, to watch Jesus as he slept.

I want to challenge you to hold this human image of Almighty God in your minds throughout our time together today. Use this fabric to help you in this: Feel its softness; smell its aroma. And at the same time, meditate upon the power, strength, and sovereignty of Christ the Lord.

Then continue your sermon as planned.

57

Go! Fight! Win!

Risk Rating: Medium

Scripture: 1 Corinthians 9:24-27

Key Verse: "Run to win" (1 Corinthians 9:24b).

Theme: Super Bowl Sunday

Point: Spiritual growth doesn't happen by accident.

Synopsis: (for use from the pulpit) Audience members will be challenged to win a competition—without knowing how to prepare for it.

Supplies: Four medium-sized, unexpected objects such as a beach ball, a child's plush bear, a cowboy hat, and a golf club. You'll also need a watch or clock with a second hand.

Preparation: Acquire your supplies ahead of time, and pray for God to bless your teaching efforts today.

Near the beginning of your sermon, tell your audience that in honor of Super Bowl Sunday, you're going to start off the morning with a friendly little competition. Have everyone stand, and then form four teams—Team 1 being the far left section of the congregation, Team 2 being the middle-left section, Team 3 being the middle-right section, and Team 4 being the far right section. Select a captain for each team (it'll be best if each captain is near the front), and ask those captains to join you at the front of the room.

Give each captain one of the unusual objects you've brought—but don't give any explanation for it. If time permits and if your congregation is comfortable with this kind of vocal outburst, have each team practice a victory cheer led by its captain. Then send the captains back to their teams and say:

All right! You all seem to be ready, so we'll get started. The team that scores the most points within 30 seconds wins. Ready? Go!

Don't give any additional directions, just start timing 30 seconds. Obviously, your congregants will be confused (since you didn't give them any real instructions for the competition). Most likely they will simply stand around wondering what to do. Feel free to add to their confusion by exhorting teams to "get busy" or to "hurry up, time is running out!" Count down the last 10 seconds in dramatic fashion, and then turn to the captains and ask them to report how many points their respective teams scored. Of course, none of the teams will have scored any points because you didn't give them any directions on *how* points could be scored.

When everyone is thoroughly confused (and possibly a little frustrated at you!), collect your props from the captains, and have everyone sit down. Then say:

Let's take a moment to talk about what we just experienced.

> **Tip**
>
> If you have a particularly competitive (and inventive) captain, he or she may try to bluff you by reporting that his or her team scored many points. Be sure to call that person's bluff in a friendly but firm way. Point out that you closely observed the team's behavior during the competition and—in spite of the fact that they clearly had winning talent on the team—they did nothing with it and managed to score no points.

Ask congregants to turn to someone nearby and discuss these questions:

• *What went through your mind when you were asked to score points for your team but were given no idea of how to score?*

• *What emotions did you feel as the 30 seconds of the game were being counted down?*

• *What would have helped your team to be more prepared for this competition?*

• *What might we learn from this experience that could help us prepare for spiritual victories in our daily lives?*

After allowing time for people to discuss their responses to the questions, invite a few volunteers to share insights from their discussions. Then read aloud 1 Corinthians 9:24-27, and say:

*Sometimes we approach our own spiritual growth with the same lacka-daisical attitude toward preparation that we experienced in this morning's team competition—and then we seem surprised by the shortage of spiritual victories we experience in daily life. Just as the two teams playing in today's Super Bowl didn't simply luck their way into the big game, we must realize that **spiritual growth doesn't happen by accident.** Perhaps we'd be wiser to take the Apostle Paul's advice in 1 Corinthians 9:24 and "run to win," dili-gently preparing ourselves each day to triumph over the trials and tempta-tions that are certain to come our way today, tomorrow, and beyond.*

Then continue your sermon as planned.

Communion Bread Bakers

Risk Rating: High

Scripture: 1 Corinthians 11:23-26

Key Verse: "This is my body, which is given for you" (1 Corinthians 11:24b).

Theme: Maundy Thursday or the Lord's Supper

Point: As leaders in our church, we have a unique opportunity to serve our people during the celebration of the Lord's Supper.

Synopsis: (for use in a staff meeting) Staff members will cook bread to be used by the congregation in celebration of the Lord's Supper.

Supplies: An oven (either in a home or at the church), the ingredients and utensils indicated in the bread recipe on page 162, and other Lord's Supper elements

Preparation: Acquire your supplies ahead of time, and pray for God to bless your teaching efforts today.

Next time you are planning to administer the Lord's Supper to your congregation (such as during a regular Lord's Supper time or at a Maundy Thursday service), ask your pastoral staff members to offer a unique service to your people by hand-baking the bread ahead of time.

A day before the planned Lord's Supper service, gather your staff members in a kitchen. You may want to provide an assortment of snacks for your staff members to munch on as you work together.

Read 1 Corinthians 11:23-26 aloud; then say:

Tomorrow we will be fulfilling this Scripture when we observe the Lord's Supper with our full congregation. ***As leaders in our church, we have a***

unique opportunity to serve our people during the celebration of the Lord's Supper. So, as a special service to our church, we are going to take time today to bake—from scratch!—the bread we will use during tomorrow's service.

Lead your team in a short prayer, thanking God for his sacrifice and asking for his blessing on your time of service together. Then get busy baking! Decide how many loaves you'll make. (One option is to make a large batch and then freeze any leftovers for future use.) Divide the labor responsibilities among your staff members—but insist that everyone participate, regardless of his or her "kitchen skills." Keep the tone light and friendly, but also help your staff work with careful attention to making the best bread possible for the coming service. Be careful not to bake the bread too long, or it might be too hard or crumbly for use. Use the recipe for "Lisa's Famous Communion Bread" below as your baking guide.

When the bread is done, congratulate participants on their efforts and then, as a service to them, use the freshly baked bread to administer the Lord's Supper to each individual on your staff. Package the rest of the bread for storage until tomorrow's church service.

Lisa's Famous Communion Bread

Melt and heat together:
4 tablespoons butter
¾ cup milk
2 tablespoons honey

Mix in: 1 ½ cups whole wheat flour
½ cup white flour
1 teaspoon salt
1 teaspoon sugar
1 teaspoon baking powder

Mix by hand until well blended. Place half of mixture on floured surface. Knead until it's not grainy (about 1 minute). Roll out to about ⅛-inch thick. Transfer to cookie sheet. Use a pizza cutter to cut into bite-sized pieces. Bake at 375 degrees for 5 minutes. Turn pan in oven and bake another 5 minutes. Repeat with other half of dough. Cool completely before packaging for storage.
YIELD: About 450 small pieces.

59

Sweet Hearts

Risk Rating: Medium

Scripture: 1 Corinthians 13:1-13

Key Verse: "The greatest of these is love"
(1 Corinthians 13:13b).

Theme: Valentine's Day

Point: God's love fits every description of love.

Synopsis: (for use in an adult small group or Sunday school class) Learners will use candy conversation hearts to spark memories of love.

Supplies: A candy conversation heart for each participant

Preparation: Acquire your supplies ahead of time, and prior to your meeting have someone remove any of the candy hearts that bear inappropriate or risqué messages. You'll be using the hearts to form pairs, so make sure that every message you include is represented on two hearts. Pray for God to bless your teaching efforts today.

What could be more appropriate for a Valentine's Day teaching idea than the "love chapter" of the Bible, 1 Corinthians 13? At the point during which you're ready to use this idea, distribute the candy hearts to everyone in the group. Say:

This Valentine's Day, let's take a little time to reflect on our experiences of love. First, read the phrase on your candy heart. Then find another person who has the same phrase on his or her heart, and form a pair with that person.

Allow a moment for people with the same phrases to find each other and form pairs. Then instruct all groups to read 1 Corinthians 13:1-13 together. Say:

After you've read this passage, tell your partner about a time someone showed you the kind of love these verses describe. Then brainstorm together to come up with a "candy heart" phrase to describe that situation.

Allow several minutes for sharing. Then have pairs join to form foursomes, and have group members take turns reporting the examples of love and its accompanying candy heart phrase to their new partners. Then say:

*This year, let's have Valentine's Day remind us not only of the love people have shown us but also of the love God has shown us. **God's love fits every description of love** in this passage. God's love is perfect, and best of all, God's love never ends.*

Continue your lesson, challenging group members to think during the coming week about times God has shown his perfect love to them.

60

Photo Gallery of Easter in Action

Risk Rating: High

Scripture: 1 Corinthians 15:1-8

Key Verse: "He was buried, and he was raised from the dead on the third day, just as the Scriptures said" (1 Corinthians 15:4).

Theme: Easter

Point: This Easter we celebrate and commemorate the awesome work of Jesus Christ.

Synopsis: (for use with an adult small group or Sunday school class) Learners will capture on film your church's celebrations surrounding Easter and, from that, create a photo gallery.

Supplies: Cameras (digital or 35mm) and film (if necessary). You'll want to recruit group members to donate cameras for use in this activity. You'll also need a way to print out and/or develop pictures, a large poster board to display your photo gallery, and glue or tape to affix pictures on the poster board.

Preparation: Acquire your supplies ahead of time, and pray for God to bless your teaching efforts. Also, be aware that this celebratory project will take at least two small-group or Sunday school class meetings to complete, and help your learners prepare for that.

During a small-group meeting or Sunday school class shortly before Palm Sunday or Easter, ask volunteers to make cameras available (and film, if necessary) for your group to use. One camera for every two people should be plenty.

Have everyone read aloud (in unison) 1 Corinthians 15:1-8, which is a powerful, succinct testimony of Christ's death and resurrection. Then say:

This Easter we celebrate and commemorate the awesome work of Jesus Christ *that is described in this passage. As a special celebration, our group is going to create a photo gallery of Easter in action at our church.*

Form pairs, and make sure each pair has access to a camera. Then have your fledgling photojournalists choose a day in the coming week when your church will be in session and celebrating the Easter season. This could be a Sunday morning or a midweek night when several groups are meeting.

Once you have chosen the date and time, encourage your group members to meet their partners at the church on that date and walk around the church in pairs taking pictures of your church members as they celebrate the Easter season. For instance, photo teams might take pictures of stage hands setting up for an Easter musical, a youth group singing worship songs, people enjoying a midweek potluck, or children waving palm branches. Remind group members that the key phrase is "Easter in Action"—meaning they want to capture on film the way your church is participating in the celebration of the Resurrection. Have your photo teams develop their pictures and bring them to your next small-group meeting or Sunday school class.

At that meeting, have your group members share their pictures with one another and then use the poster board to create a joyful display titled "A Photo Gallery of Easter in Action." Display the poster board prominently in your church lobby for a month or so after the holiday to let your church members enjoy the reminder of their Easter celebration.

61

Absurd but True

Risk Rating: Low

Scripture: 1 Corinthians 15:12-23

Key Verse: "In fact, Christ has been raised from the dead" (1 Corinthians 15:20a).

Theme: Easter

Point: The fact is that Christ has been raised from the dead.

Synopsis: (for use from the pulpit) Participants will examine watermelon seeds as an illustration of God's redemptive thinking.

Supplies: A watermelon seed for each participant

Preparation: Acquire your supplies ahead of time (watermelon seeds are easily obtainable during springtime at most lawn and garden stores), and pray for God to bless your teaching efforts today.

This interactive experience illustrates that God's redemptive plan for us often goes far beyond the logic of our rational and finite minds.

At an appropriate time during your sermon, ask the ushers to distribute watermelon seeds to everyone in the congregation. (Filling offering plates with seeds and passing them up and down the pews is an easy way to do this.) When everyone has a watermelon seed, give folks a moment to examine the tiny black seeds they hold. Then ask anyone who has ever grown watermelons in a garden to raise his or her hand. Next, ask if anyone knows the average weight of a full-grown watermelon. (It is 15 to 30 pounds!)

Ask congregation members to stand if they believe a tiny watermelon seed could actually grow to be a melon of 15 to 30 pounds. Then say:

Wait a minute. That doesn't make any sense! Are you saying that, if it is properly nourished and cared for, that little black seed you hold in your hands could actually grow to 30 pounds in the course of a few months? Absurd!

Pause for a moment; then ask the congregation to be seated. Then say:

At first it does seem irrational and impossible for a tiny black seed to grow into a large, delicious watermelon. But we all have some measure of experience with watermelons, and we know beyond a doubt that this truly happens.

Read aloud 1 Corinthians 15:12-23; then say:

To many people, even in his own day and especially in ours, the Apostle Paul's assertions in this passage seemed irrational, illogical, and absurd! A man raised from the dead? Seems impossible, but as verse 20 so eloquently says, "In fact, Christ has been raised from the dead." And that is what we are here to celebrate today.

Continue your sermon as planned.

Get Off My Pew!

Risk Rating: Medium

Scripture: 2 Corinthians 5:17

Key Verse: "New life has begun!"
(2 Corinthians 5:17b).

Theme: Autumn

Point: Change is the tool God uses to bring us new life and strengthen our faith.

Synopsis: (for use from the pulpit) Participants will change seats unexpectedly.

Supplies: Photocopies of the "Get Off My Pew!" discussion questions (p.171) and cellophane tape

Preparation: Before your church service, photocopy the "Get Off My Pew!" discussion questions (p.171), and tape a copy under both ends of each pew or row in your auditorium. Pray for God to bless your teaching efforts today.

Use this activity when summer begins changing to autumn to help congregation members learn how God uses change to bring new life into his people. At the appropriate time during your sermon, say:

We are now in a season of change. Summer is giving way to fall. Autumn leaves are changing color and falling to the ground. The weather is getting colder; summer vacations are over. Old things are passing away in preparation for becoming new next spring. And now it's time for another change right here in our auditorium.

Have everyone stand and gather his or her belongings. Then say:

Please move to the pew to your right. Those on the far right side of the

room, please cross over and sit in a pew on the far left.

After everyone has changed places, instruct members of the congregation to form groups of five to eight (while remaining in their rows).

Tip

If the people in your care are genuinely opposed to talking with others during church, then feel free to ask your congregants to quietly reflect on the discussion questions individually instead of talking about them with a partner or small group. In this situation, you'll want to display a PowerPoint slide or overhead transparency of the discussion questions for the whole congregation instead of taping copies of the questions under the pews.

Have each group remove the discussion questions from under the end of the pew and share responses to the questions with one another. After discussion time, ask the questions again from the pulpit, one at a time, and allow several groups to share the results of their discussions.

Afterward, read 2 Corinthians 5:17 aloud; then say:

A change of seasons, a change of seats, and changes in life are sometimes difficult to face. But as 2 Corinthians 5:17 reminds us, **change is the tool God uses to bring us new life and strengthen our faith** *as we daily grow closer to him.*

Then continue your sermon as planned.

"Get Off My Pew!" Discussion Questions

- What feelings did you have when you were asked to change seats? Explain.

- How do you react when you face changes in real life? Explain.

- When did a change in your life strengthen your faith in God?

"Get Off My Pew!" Discussion Questions

- What feelings did you have when you were asked to change seats? Explain.

- How do you react when you face changes in real life? Explain.

- When did a change in your life strengthen your faith in God?

Permission to photocopy this handout from *Make It Stick* granted for local church use. Copyright © Group Publishing, Inc., P.O. Box 481, Loveland, CO 80539. www.group.com

63

No Random Gift

Risk Rating: Low

Scripture: 2 Corinthians 9:15

Key Verse: "Thank God for this gift too wonderful for words!" (2 Corinthians 9:15).

Theme: Christmas

Point: The gift of God's Son that very first Christmas was given to you, to me, and to the whole world.

Synopsis: (for use from the pulpit) Congregation members will participate in a random gift-giving experience.

Supplies: A small present that would be enjoyed by any member of your congregation (such as a gift certificate to a local restaurant or department store), one photocopy of "Gift-Giving Directions" (p.174), and a hat

Preparation: Acquire your gift, and wrap it in bright Christmas paper. Photocopy the "Gift-Giving Directions" (p.174), and cut the copy into appropriate strips (one gift-giving direction per strip). Place those strips in a hat so they can be drawn out at random, and place the hat near the place you'll deliver your sermon. Pray for God to bless your teaching efforts today.

The birth of Christ is commonly celebrated by giving gifts to those we love. Use this idea to remind congregation members that Jesus was the first and best Christmas present ever. At the appropriate time during your sermon, read aloud 2 Corinthians 9:15. Then tell everyone that in celebration of this verse and of the season, you, too, have decided to give a gift.

Show everyone the wrapped gift you prepared; then give it to someone in your congregation. Tell people that the gift can't be opened yet. Then show everyone the hat with the gift-giving directions in it. Explain that each slip of paper contains a direction that must be followed before the gift can be opened. Then draw one of the slips of paper (or have a volunteer draw it), and read the directions.

Have your congregation move the gift as indicated; then draw a new slip of paper. Continue as time allows or until you run out of directions. Have the last person to hold the gift open it and tell everyone what he or she has received. Let this person know that he or she may keep the gift. Then say:

*It's fun to randomly give and receive a gift like this one. But this Christmas, let's remember that Jesus' birth wasn't a random present for some lucky person who just happened to be sitting in the right seat. **The gift of God's Son that very first Christmas was given to you, to me, and to the whole world.** And as 2 Corinthians 9:15 reminds us, that was a gift that is truly too wonderful for words!*

Continue your sermon, encouraging people to personally receive the greatest gift ever this Christmas season.

Gift-Giving Directions

Photocopy this handout, and then cut along the dotted lines to create separate strips of paper. Feel free to adapt the specific directions to better fit your location and congregation.

- -

Move the gift three people to the right.

- -

Move the gift 10 people back.

- -

Move the gift three people forward and then one person toward the nearest wall.

- -

Move the gift four people in the direction of the piano.

- -

Move the gift eight people forward, then three people back.

- -

Move the gift to the closest person wearing red earrings.

- -

Move the gift to the closest person wearing a green shirt.

- -

Move the gift randomly so 15 different people touch it at least once—and only once.

- -

64

Free at Last

Risk Rating: Medium

Scripture: Galatians 4:4-7

Key Verse: "God sent [his Son] to buy freedom for us" (Galatians 4:5a).

Theme: Independence Day

Point: We can share in the freedom that Christ brings.

Synopsis: (for use from the pulpit) Participants will feel trapped by crepe paper barriers.

Supplies: Tape and several rolls of colored crepe paper—enough to make several barriers on each side of each row, preventing the people in the pews from getting out.

Preparation: Acquire your supplies ahead of time, and leave your crepe paper rolls at the back of the church, ready for use. You'll need to recruit several ushers or other assistants to help you with this exercise as well. Explain to them that when you give the signal (such as a nod of the head), they're to move from the back of the church to the front of the church, unwinding the crepe paper and taping three or four rows of steamers along the sides of the pews or seats as they go. The result should be a streamer "fence" that leaves people "trapped" in their seats. Also, pray for God to bless your teaching efforts today.

At the appropriate time during your sermon, address the celebration of Independence Day and the freedom our nation won during the Revolutionary War. Then use this experience to help your congregation move beyond the discussion of our country's freedom to the freedom Christians have through Jesus.

At the appropriate time during your sermon, secretly cue your assistants to begin creating the streamer "fence" along the edges of the pews. Ignore them as they work, continuing with your sermon as if nothing is happening in the auditorium. When everyone is "fenced in," continue speaking a few more minutes, letting people wonder why they've been blocked from exiting. During this time, read aloud Galatians 4:4-7, emphasizing verse 5 and the freedom from legalism and punishment that Christ provides for us. When you're ready, say:

Turn to someone near you, and describe your thoughts as you were fenced into your pew today.

If time allows, invite several volunteers to share their thoughts with the congregation as a whole. Then continue your sermon on Galatians 4:4-7, comparing being trapped in sin to being trapped in the pew. Leave the streamers up for the entire sermon.

End your message by declaring the freedom Christ bought with his death and resurrection. Then dismiss the congregation by saying:

*As a symbol that **we can share in the freedom that Christ brings**, I invite you to break through the streamers at the end of your row right now—and let this begin your celebration of Independence Day this year!*

Afterward, join with your assistants in cleaning up the torn streamers all over your auditorium.

65

Wedded Bliss

Risk Rating: Low

Scripture: Ephesians 5:21-33

Key Verse: "Submit to one another out of reverence for Christ" (Ephesians 5:21).

Theme: Weddings

Point: Submit to one another out of reverence for Christ.

Synopsis: (for use from the pulpit) Audience members will expand on Paul's advice for a strong marriage.

Supplies: A pen and a heart-shaped paper for each wedding guest and a few baskets

Preparation: Acquire heart-shaped papers ahead of time. You may want to cut these hearts yourself, or you can purchase them at a stationery or specialty-paper store. Before the wedding ceremony, place a basket near each exit. Pray for God to bless your teaching efforts today.

During the wedding ceremony, as you are addressing the couple to be married and their guests, say to the bride and groom:

In Ephesians 5:21-33, the Apostle Paul gives us great advice for building a strong, lasting, and Christ-honoring marriage. **Submit to one another out of reverence for Christ.** *Put your spouse before yourself. Love each other. Respect each other.*

Read aloud the full passage of Ephesians 5:21-33. Then say to the audience:

Think about the advice you might give to this couple to help them put into

practice Paul's instructions to love and respect each other and thus build a strong, lasting, Christ-honoring marriage.

After a moment of "think time," have ushers distribute the paper hearts and pens. Say:

Write your words of advice to our bride and groom today on this heart-shaped paper.

Tell the wedding guests that their advice will be bound into a booklet and will be given to the bride and groom as a practical reminder of the Bible's instructions on marriage. Then allow a moment or two for people to write their advice.

When everyone is finished, instruct the wedding guests to drop their written advice in the baskets near the exit doors. Then continue with the wedding ceremony.

Afterward, have the heart-shaped papers made into a booklet for the bride and groom. This can be done by having a print shop drill a hole into the stack of hearts and tying a ribbon through the hole. Deliver the booklet to the newlyweds when they return from their honeymoon.

Tip

You'll probably please the bride and groom if the paper you select for this activity matches their choice of colors for the wedding!

Tip

If possible, you may want to display the text of Ephesians 5:21-33 on a PowerPoint slide or overhead transparency so that audience members may refer to it as they write their advice.

66

Three Amigos

Risk Rating: Low

Scripture: Ephesians 6:2-3

Key Verse: "Honor your father and mother" (Ephesians 6:2a).

Theme: Mother's Day or Father's Day

Point: Parents are real-life heroes.

Synopsis: (for use from the pulpit) Audience members will view and reflect on a clip from the film *Three Amigos*.

Supplies: A DVD version of the 1986 film *Three Amigos* (rated PG, starring Steve Martin, Martin Short, and Chevy Chase) and the ability to show a clip from this DVD to the congregation

Preparation: Acquire your supplies ahead of time, and pray for God to bless your teaching efforts today. The film clip for this experience is located in tracks 2 and 3 on the DVD, beginning about three minutes from the start of the movie. This specific clip runs from time counter point 0:03:00 (the beginning of track 2) through 0:11:08 (the end of track 3). Please be sure to preview this clip to make sure its content is appropriate for your congregation.

At the appropriate time during your sermon, introduce the DVD clip from *Three Amigos* by saying:

In 1986, Steve Martin, Martin Short, and Chevy Chase starred in Three Amigos, *a now-classic comedy about three out-of-work actors and their hilarious exploits in the real world.*

The three main characters in this movie are actors in a series of silent films about the Wild West. But when they ask for a raise, their studio bosses unceremoniously fire them. Meanwhile, a real bandito and his gang are terrorizing people who live in a small Mexican village. Not knowing that the three amigos are only actors, one woman calls upon them to save the village from the evil El Guapo. The amigos think they are simply being asked to do a live performance of their show, and they accept. As you can guess, hijinks ensue. Let's watch a scene from this movie now...

After the clip, ask these questions:

• *Were these guys real heroes? Why or why not?*

• *What does it take to be a real hero?*

• *Do you know any people you consider heroes? What makes them heroic in your eyes?*

Say:

*No discussion of heroes is complete without mentioning parents. After all, **parents are real-life heroes** in this world of ours—and they deserve to be treated as such.*

Read aloud Ephesians 6:2-3. Then ask:

• *In what ways would you say that parents are real heroes?*

• *Why do you suppose Scripture instructs us to honor our parents—heroes or not?*

• *When was the last time you honored your parents as heroes?*

• *What can we do today to honor our parents? What can we do next week? six months from now?*

After allowing congregation members to reflect on these questions, continue your sermon as planned.

IDEA 67

Dressed for Winter

Risk Rating: Low

Scripture: Ephesians 6:10-20

Key Verse: "Put on all of God's armor"
(Ephesians 6:11a).

Theme: Winter

Point: God has provided spiritual clothing to protect us against the forces of evil.

Synopsis: (for use from the pulpit) Audience members will compare winter clothing to the armor of God.

Supplies: None

Preparation: Plan to use this activity on a cold winter day when your congregation will likely be layered in all kinds of protective coats, sweaters, gloves, and the like. Pray for God to bless your teaching efforts today.

As you begin your sermon, instruct congregation members to stand and put on anything and everything they might have brought as protection against the cold. Suggest that they don items such as sweaters, gloves, scarves, hats, coats, and so on, just as if they were about to go back outside into the frigid weather. When everyone is all bundled up, say:

Look around at what everyone is wearing. This protective winter clothing is the closest thing to armor that most of us wear, and this is how we dress to battle the forces of nature during the icy winter days. Each day the tempera-ture dips, we are almost fanatical about covering as much of our bodies as possible in order to protect ourselves from the cold.

Thank congregation members for their participation, and then allow people to remove their outerwear as they return to their seats. Say:

Just as we wear specific kinds of clothing to protect us from the forces of nature during the winter, **God has provided spiritual clothing to protect us against the forces of evil** *every day of our lives. Let's read about that right now.*

Read aloud Ephesians 6:10-20; then continue your sermon as planned. As you speak about the various parts of God's spiritual armor, compare them to various items worn or used during nasty weather. For example, an umbrella might be compared to the shield of faith, and snow boots might represent feet wearing the good news of peace.

Tip

If it would be too difficult for the entire congregation to put on their coats and such, choose three or four volunteers and send them out during the sermon to get their coats and other outerwear and model them for the congregation.

Spring-Cleaning for the Soul

Risk Rating: Low

Scripture: Philippians 2:14-15

Key Verse: "Live clean, innocent lives as children of God" (Philippians 2:15b).

Theme: Spring

Point: While we clean our homes this spring, let's also focus on living "clean, innocent lives as children of God."

Synopsis: (for use from the pulpit) Audience members will clean up a cluttered auditorium as a reminder to spring-clean the soul.

Supplies: Believe it or not, you'll need a little "clutter" for this experience!

Preparation: During the week before your sermon, give the church custodian a break. Leave the papers, hymnals, Bibles, bulletins, and other odds and ends that are often left after a service right where they are. In fact, if your congregation isn't messy enough, stop by the auditorium the night before your sermon and do a bit of "cluttering" yourself. Also, pray for God to bless your teaching efforts today.

As you begin your sermon, point out that spring is often a time of cleaning. We clear out the winter dust and cobwebs, then open the windows to let in fresh, clean air. Next comment on the untidiness of your auditorium and ask everyone to pitch in and help spring-clean the sanctuary.

Have congregation members pick up bits of trash and old bulletins. Send ushers or other assistants around with trash bags. Ask people to return songbooks or Bibles to the pew racks, and to put any other item (such as pencils, pens, and visitor cards) into their proper places as well. After cleanup is done (or after a few minutes of spring cleaning), have people stop what they're doing and return to their seats. Say:

Look around and see how nice this room looks now. It was easy to clean our sanctuary in just a short time, which is to be expected since most of us probably grew up believing that the statement "Cleanliness is next to godliness" came straight out of the Bible—even though it didn't. Still, cleanliness is nice, and the Bible does speak about this issue, but in a different context. Let's read about that now.

Read aloud Philippians 2:14-15, emphasizing the exhortation to "live clean, innocent lives as children of God" in verse 15. Say:

Cleaning is a normal part of this season. So, **while we clean our homes this spring, let's also focus on living "clean, innocent lives as children of God"** *as Philippians 2:15 encourages us to do.*

Continue your sermon as planned.

69

Happy New Life

Risk Rating: Medium

Scripture: Colossians 3:1-10

Key Verse: "You have been raised to new life with Christ" (Colossians 3:1a).

Theme: New Year's Day

Point: God makes us entirely new from the inside out.

Synopsis: (for use in an adult small group or Sunday school class) Learners will form new sculptures out of old ones.

Supplies: A small sheet of foil (about 6 inches square) for each participant

Preparation: Acquire your supplies ahead of time, and pray for God to bless your teaching efforts today.

At the appropriate time during your small-group or Sunday school lesson, distribute a sheet of foil to each person. Say:

Each New Year's holiday, we traditionally look for ways to change bad habits from our past and create a new hope for the future. We turn over a new leaf, renew our resolutions, and make plans for the things we'd like to accomplish in the coming year.

Right now, I'd like us to examine this idea of newness that comes with a new year. I'd like you to take the foil you're holding and create something entirely new from it. Reshape it into an airplane, an animal, a hat, or whatever you want.

After about two minutes, have each person join with another member of the group to form pairs (or a group of three, if necessary). Have each person share his or her new creation with a partner and, if necessary, explain what it is. Then say:

Now I'd like you to somehow join your creation with that of your partner(s) to make another, entirely new, object. This may require some reshaping of the foil, but do what's necessary to create something new.

Allow a minute or two for pairs to do this. Have a few groups who are especially pleased with their results share them with the larger group. Then collect all the foil sculptures, and explain that all of these new creations will again be reshaped as they are recycled and made into new aluminum products. Then have partners read Colossians 3:1-10 in their pairs and briefly discuss these questions:

• *How is the way we reshaped our foil sheets like the way we're reshaped by God into new life? How is it different?*

• *In what ways is God reshaping us into new life right now?*

After discussions, allow time for volunteers from each pair to share highlights of their responses. Then say:

We've reshaped our used bits of foil to create new images, but God does more than simply reshape or recycle us. **God makes us entirely new from the inside out.**

Continue your lesson, exploring God's creative, life-giving work as it's described in Colossians 3:1-10.

70

God's Rest

Risk Rating: Medium

Scripture: 2 Thessalonians 1:7

Key Verse: "God will provide rest for you"
(2 Thessalonians 1:7a).

Theme: Summer

Point: We can be confident that God will keep his promise of rest for those who place their faith in Jesus.

Synopsis: (for use from the pulpit) Participants will take a rest break during church.

Supplies: None

Preparation: Pray for God to bless your teaching efforts today.

Before reading today's Scripture text for your sermon, tell people to get as comfortable as they possibly can. Encourage them to recline, lean on the shoulders of others near them (with permission, of course), put up their feet, loosen their ties, take off their shoes, even stretch out in the aisle if they like. When people are relaxed, ask them to close their eyes and listen to you. Say:

This life we lead as Christians isn't easy. It seems each day that more and more people set out to oppose Jesus and to antagonize his followers. Every day brings news of Christians being persecuted in nations all over the world. Some are physically harmed; others of us are economically, socially, or emotionally harmed. It can get overwhelming dealing with the hateful and mocking attitudes of the media, our neighbors, and governments.

But it's summertime now, and summer brings with it a reminder of rest. Kids are out of school. The hammock and a tall glass of lemonade beckon. Lazy days at a beach or swimming pool are within reach. Many of us are blessed with time off from work, with a little vacation or a trip to a nice place. The best thing about summer, however, is that these rare, restful moments we experience now are gentle reminders of the great, soul-regenerating, eternal-life rest that God promises to deliver to us one fine day. Listen to what the Bible says about that.

Read aloud 2 Thessalonians 1:7, with emphasis on the first half of the verse. If appropriate read it twice to help its message sink in. Then ask congregation members to open their eyes and return to their normal seated positions. Have everyone find a partner nearby and discuss these questions:

• *What's the most restful aspect of summertime for you?*

• *What feelings did you have as you heard about God's promise of rest for you while you were relaxing here today?*

• *What's most appealing to you about the prospect of entering God's rest?*

• *What do you think God's rest will be like?*

After discussions, say:

Although we can't completely escape persecution for our belief in Jesus while we live in this world, and although we can't be exactly sure of what God's rest will look like, **we can be confident that God will keep his promise of rest for those who place their faith in Jesus.**

Then continue your sermon as planned.

index

risk rating index

low risk index

medium risk index

high risk index

theme index

scripture index